To Gram
Love Chris
mar/86

Favorite Poems in Large Print

Favorite Poems
in Large Print

Edited by Virginia S. Reiser

Boston, Massachusetts

1981

Library of Congress Cataloging in Publication Data

Main entry under title:

Favorite poems in large print.

1. American poetry. 2. English poetry.
3. Large type books. I. Reiser, Virginia.
[PS583.F3]   811'.008   80-29407
ISBN 0-8161-3160-0   (l. print)

© 1981 G. K. Hall & Co.

Illustrations © 1981 by Sheryl White

Set in Penta / Mergenthaler Linotron 202
16 pt Times Roman

Acknowledgments

The editor gratefully acknowledges permission to reproduce copyright poems in this book.

Rupert Brooke: "Day That I Have Loved," "The Great Lover" and "The Soldier" from *The Collected Poems of Rupert Brooke* reprinted by permission of Dodd, Mead & Company, Inc. Copyright 1915 by Dodd, Mead & Company, Inc. Copyright renewed 1943 by Edward Marsh. Reprinted by permission of the Canadian publishers, McClelland and Stewart Limited, Toronto.

G. K. Chesterton: "The Donkey" and "A Prayer in Darkness" by permission of The Estate of G. K. Chesterton and J.M. Dent & Sons Ltd.

e e cummings: "anyone lived in a pretty how town," copyright 1940 by E.E. Cummings; copyright 1968 by Marion Morehouse Cummings. Reprinted from *Complete Poems 1913–1962* by E.E. Cummings by permission of Harcourt Brace Jovanovich, Inc.

Emily Dickinson: "Because I Could Not Stop for Death," "The Bustle in a House," "I Had No Time to Hate," "I Never Saw a Moor," "I've Seen a Dying Eye," "If I Can Stop One Heart from Breaking," "A Narrow Fellow in the Grass," "Success Is Counted Sweetest" and "There Is No Frigate Like a Book" reprinted by permission of the publishers and the Trustees of Amherst College from *The Poems of Emily Dickinson*, edited by Thomas H. Johnson, Cambridge, Mass.: The Belknap Press of Harvard University Press, Copyright © 1951, 1955, 1979 by the President and Fellows of Harvard College.

Robert Frost: "Acquainted with the Night," "After Apple Picking," "Birches," "Fire and Ice," "Mending Wall," "The Road Not Taken" and "Stopping By Woods on a Snowy Evening" from *The Poetry of Robert Frost* edited by Edward Connery Lathem. Copyright 1916, 1923, 1928, 1930, 1939, © 1969 by Holt, Rinehart and Winston. Copyright 1944, 1951, © 1956, 1958 by Robert Frost. Copyright © 1967 by Lesley Frost Ballantine. Reprinted by permission of Holt, Rinehart and Winston, Publishers.

Edgar A. Guest: "It Couldn't Be Done" reprinted from *Collected Verse of Edgar A. Guest* by Edgar A. Guest, © 1934 with the permission of Contemporary Books, Inc., Chicago.

For H.F.R.

Contents

Love and Friendship

Nature and the Seasons

Childhood and Youth

Grief and Death

Patriotism and War

Faith and Inspiration

Reflection and Contemplation

Humor

Various Themes

Introduction

Many readers have written to me saying that there is no poetry readily available in Large Print. Often they mention favorite poems that they would enjoy rereading — if only they could. In compiling the 267 poems in this book, I have tried to answer this need by including poems mentioned by readers, poems in our collective memories, and poems that I find myself turning to again and again.

I hope these poems of love, friendship, humor, inspiration, storytelling, and more will bring back the joy of poetry to all Large Print readers. For the reader's convenience, the poems are arranged in categories, chronologically within each category.

I would like to take this opportunity to express my appreciation to all who helped in producing this anthology. To Anne McLaurin, Eliza Lewis, Cindy Schrom, and Pat Hutchinson, my deepest thanks.

Virginia S. Reiser
Boston, Mass.

Stories and Ballads

Lord Randal

"O where hae ye been, Lord Randal, my
    son?
O where hae ye been, my handsome young
    man?"
"I hae been to the wild wood; mother, make
    my bed soon,
For I'm weary wi hunting, and fain wald lie
    down."

"Where gat ye your dinner, Lord Randal, my
    son?
Where gat ye your dinner, my handsome
    young man?"
"I din'd wi my true-love; mother, make my
    bed soon,
For I'm weary wi hunting, and fain wald lie
    down."

"What gat ye to your dinner, Lord Randal, my
    son?
What gat ye to your dinner, my handsome
    young man?"
"I gat eels boiled in broo; mother, make my
    bed soon,

For I'm weary wi hunting, and fain wald lie
    down.''

"What became of your bloodhounds, Lord
    Randal, my son?
What became of your bloodhounds, my
    handsome young man?''
"O they swelld and they died; mother, make
    my bed soon,
For I'm weary wi hunting, and fain wald lie
    down.''

"O I fear ye are poisond, Lord Randal, my
    son!
O I fear ye are poisond, my handsome young
    man!''
"O yes! I am poisond; mother, make my bed
    soon,
For I'm sick at the heart, and I fain wald lie
    down.''

Unknown

Lochinvar

Oh, young Lochinvar is come out of the west:
Through all the wide border his steed was the
    best;
And save his good broadsword he weapons had
    none;

He rode all unarmed and he rode all alone.
So faithful in love, and so dauntless in war,
There never was knight like young Lochinvar!

He stayed not for brake, and he stopped not for
  stone;
He swam the Esk River where ford there was
  none:
But ere he alighted at Netherby gate,
The bride had consented, the gallant came late;
For a laggard in love, and a dastard in war,
Was to wed the fair Ellen of brave Lochinvar.

So boldly he entered the Netherby Hall,
Among bride'smen, and kinsmen, and
  brothers, and all:
Then spoke the bride's father, his hand on his
  sword
(For the poor craven bridegroom said never a
  word),
"O come ye in peace here, or come ye in war,
Or to dance at our bridal, young Lord
  Lochinvar?" —

"I long wooed your daughter, my suit you
  denied; —
Love swells like the Solway, but ebbs like its
  tide!
And now am I come, with this lost love of
  mine,

To lead but one measure, drink one cup of
    wine:
There are maidens in Scotland more lovely by
    far,
That would gladly be bride to the young
    Lochinvar.''

The bride kissed the goblet; the knight took it
    up,
He quaffed off the wine, and he threw down
    the cup.
She looked down to blush, and she looked up
    to sigh,
With a smile on her lips, and a tear in her eye.
He took her soft hand, ere her mother could
    bar, —
''Now tread me a measure!'' said young
    Lochinvar.

So stately his form, and so lovely her face,
That never a hall such a galliard did grace:
While her mother did fret, and her father did
    fume,
And the bridegroom stood dangling his bonnet
    and plume;
And the bride-maidens whispered. '' 'T were
    better by far
To have matched our fair cousin with young
    Lochinvar.''

One touch to her hand, and one word in her
    ear,
When they reached the hall door, and the
    charger stood near;
So light to the croupe the fair lady he swung,
So light to the saddle before her he sprung!
"She is won! we are gone, over bank, bush,
    and scaur:
They'll have fleet steeds that follow," quoth
    young Lochinvar.

There was mounting 'mong Graemes of the
    Netherby clan:
Forsters, Fenwicks, and Musgraves, they rode
    and they ran;
There was racing and chasing on Canobie Lee,
But the lost bride of Netherby ne'er did they
    see.
So daring in love, and so dauntless in war,
Have ye e'er heard of gallant like young
    Lochinvar?

Sir Walter Scott

Abou Ben Adhem

Abou Ben Adhem (may his tribe increase!)
Awoke one night from a deep dream of peace,
And saw, within the moonlight of his room,
Making it rich, and like a lily in bloom,

7

An Angel writing in a book of gold:
Exceeding peace had made Ben Adhem bold,
And to the Presence in the room he said,
"What writest thou?" The Vision raised its
 head,
And with a look made of all sweet accord
Answered, "The names of those who love the
 Lord."
"And is mine one?" said Abou. "Nay, not
 so,"
Replied the Angel. Abou spoke more low,
But cheerily still; and said, "I pray thee, then,
Write me as one that loves his fellow men."

The Angel wrote, and vanished. The next night
It came again with a great wakening light,
And showed the names whom love of God had
 blessed,
And, lo! Ben Adhem's name led all the rest!

Leigh Hunt

La Belle Dame Sans Merci

Oh what can ail thee, knight-at-arms!
 Alone and palely loitering?
The sedge has wither'd from the lake,
 And no birds sing.

8

Oh what can ail thee, knight-at-arms!
     So haggard and so woe-begone?
The squirrel's granary is full,
     And the harvest's done.

I see a lily on thy brow,
     With anquish moist and fever dew;
And on thy cheeks a fading rose
     Fast withereth too.

I met a lady in the mead —
     Full beautiful, a fairy's child;
Her hair was long, her foot was light,
     And her eyes were wild.

I made a garland for her head,
     And bracelets too, and fragrant zone;
She look'd at me as she did love,
     And made sweet moan.

I set her on my pacing steed,
     And nothing else saw all day long;
For sidelong would she bend, and sing
     A fairy song.

She found me roots of relish sweet,
     And honey wild, and manna dew;
And sure in language strange she said —
     "I love thee true."

She took me to her elfin grot,
  And there she wept, and sigh'd full sore;
And there I shut her wild, wild eyes
  With kisses four.

And there she lull'd me asleep;
  And there I dream'd — Ah! woe betide!
The latest dream I ever dream'd
  On the cold hill's side.

I saw pale kings and princes too —
  Pale warriors, death-pale were they all;
They cried — "La belle dame sans merci
  Hath thee in thrall!"

I saw their starved lips in the gloam,
  With horrid warning gapèd wide;
And I awoke, and found me here,
  On the cold hill's side.

And this is why I sojourn here,
  Alone and palely loitering.
Though the sedge is wither'd from the lake,
  And no birds sing.

John Keats

Casabianca

The boy stood on the burning deck,
   Whence all but him had fled;
The flame that lit the battle's wreck
   Shone round him o'er the dead.

Yet beautiful and bright he stood,
   As born to rule the storm;
A creature of heroic blood,
   A proud though childlike form.

The flames rolled on; he would not go
   Without his father's word;
That father, faint in death below,
   His voice no longer heard.

He called aloud, "Say, Father, say,
   If yet my task be done!"
He knew not that the chieftain lay
   Unconscious of his son.

"Speak, Father!" once again he cried,
   "If I may yet be gone!"
And but the booming shots replied,
   And fast the flames rolled on.

Upon his brow he felt their breath,
   And in his waving hair,

And looked from that lone post of death
  In still yet brave despair;

And shouted but once more aloud,
  "My father! must I stay?"
While o'er him fast, through sail and shroud,
  The wreathing fires made way.

They wrapt the ship in splendor wild,
  They caught the flag on high,
And streamed above the gallant child,
  Like banners in the sky.

There came a burst of thunder sound;
  The boy, — Oh! where was *he?*
Ask of the winds, that far around
  With fragments strewed the sea, —

With shroud and mast and pennon fair,
  That well had borne their part, —
But the noblest thing that perished there
  Was that young, faithful heart.

Felicia Hemans

The Raven

Once upon a midnight dreary, while I
    pondered, weak and weary,
Over many a quaint and curious volume of
    forgotten lore, —
While I nodded, nearly napping, suddenly
    there came a tapping,
As of some one gently rapping, rapping at my
    chamber door.
" 'Tis some visitor," I muttered, "tapping at
    my chamber door;
      Only this, and nothing more."

Ah, distinctly I remember, it was in the bleak
    December,
And each separate dying ember wrought its
    ghost upon the floor.
Eagerly I wished the morrow; vainly I had
    sought to borrow
From my books surcease of sorrow, — sorrow
    for the lost Lenore, —
For the rare and radiant maiden whom the
    angels named Lenore, —
      Nameless here forevermore.

And the silken, sad, uncertain rustling of each
    purple curtain
Thrilled me, — filled me with fantastic terrors
    never felt before;

So that now, to still the beating of my heart, I
   stood repeating,
" 'Tis some visitor entreating entrance at my
   chamber door, —
Some late visitor entreating entrance at my
   chamber door;
     That it is, and nothing more."

Presently my soul grew stronger; hesitating
   then no longer,
"Sir," said I, "or madam, truly your
   forgiveness I implore;
But the fact is, I was napping, and so gently
   you came rapping,
And so faintly you came tapping, tapping at
   my chamber door,
That I scarce was sure I heard you." — Here I
   opened wide the door;
     Darkness there, and nothing more.

Deep into that darkness peering, long I stood
   there, wondering, fearing,
Doubting, dreaming dreams no mortal ever
   dared to dream before;
But the silence was unbroken, and the darkness
   gave no token,
And the only word there spoken was the
   whispered word "Lenore!"
This I whispered, and an echo murmured back
   the word "Lenore!"

Merely this, and nothing more.

Back into the chamber turning, all my soul
    within me burning,
Soon again I heard a tapping, something louder
    than before:
"Surely," said I, "surely that is something at
    my window-lattice;
Let me see then what thereat is, and this
    mystery explore, —
Let my heart be still a moment, and this
    mystery explore, —
      'Tis the wind, and nothing more."

Open then I flung the shutter, when, with
    many a flirt and flutter,
In there stepped a stately raven of the saintly
    days of yore.
Not the least obeisance made he; not an instant
    stopped or stayed he,
But, with mien of lord or lady, perched above
    my chamber door, —
Perched upon a bust of Pallas, just above my
    chamber door, —
      Perched, and sat, and nothing more.

Then this ebony bird beguiling my sad fancy
    into smiling,
By the grave and stern decorum of the
    countenance it wore,

"Though thy crest be shorn and shaven,
   thou," I said, "art sure no craven;
Ghastly, grim, and ancient raven, wandering
   from the nightly shore,
Tell me what thy lordly name is on the night's
   Plutonian shore?"
     Quoth the raven, "Nevermore!"

Much I marvelled this ungainly fowl to hear
   discourse so plainly,
Though its answer little meaning, little
   relevancy bore;
For we cannot help agreeing that no living
   human being
Ever yet was blessed with seeing bird above
   his chamber door,
Bird or beast upon the sculptured bust above
   his chamber door,
     With such name as "Nevermore!"

But the raven, sitting lonely on the placid bust,
   spoke only
That one word, as if his soul in that one word
   he did outpour.
Nothing further then he uttered, — not a
   feather then he fluttered, —
Till I scarcely more than muttered, "Other
   friends have flown before, —
On the morrow he will leave me, as my hopes
   have flown before."

Then the bird said, "Nevermore!"

Startled at the stillness, broken by reply so
    aptly spoken,
"Doubtless," said I, "what it utters is its only
    stock and store,
Caught from some unhappy master, whom
    unmerciful disaster
Followed fast and followed faster, till his song
    one burden bore,
Till the dirges of his hope that melancholy
    burden bore, —
        Of 'Nevermore, — nevermore!' "

But the raven still beguiling all my sad soul
    into smiling,
Straight I wheeled a cushioned seat in front of
    bird and bust and door,
Then, upon the velvet sinking, I betook myself
    to linking
Fancy unto fancy, thinking what this ominous
    bird of yore —
What this grim, ungainly, ghastly, gaunt, and
    ominous bird of yore —
        Meant in croaking "Nevermore!"

This I sat engaged in guessing, but no syllable
    expressing
To the fowl whose fiery eyes now burned into
    my bosom's core;

This and more I sat divining, with my head at
ease reclining
On the cushion's velvet lining that the
lamplight gloating o'er,
But whose velvet violet lining, with the
lamplight gloating o'er,
She shall press — ah! nevermore!

Then methought the air grew denser, perfumed
from an unseen censer,
Swung by seraphim, whose footfalls tinkled on
the tufted floor.
"Wretch," I cried, "thy God hath lent thee,
— by these angels he hath sent thee
Respite, — respite and nepenthe from the
memories of Lenore!
Quaff, O, quaff this kind nepenthe, and forget
this lost Lenore!"
Quoth the raven, "Nevermore!"

"Prophet!" said I, "thing of evil! — prophet
still, if bird or devil!
Whether tempter sent, or whether tempest
tossed thee here ashore,
Desolate yet all undaunted, on this desert land
enchanted, —
On this home by horror haunted, — tell me
truly, I implore, —
Is there — is there balm in Gilead? — tell me,
— tell me, I implore!"

Quoth the raven, "Nevermore!"

"Prophet!" said I, "thing of evil! — prophet
    still, if bird or devil!
By that heaven that bends above us, — by that
    God we both adore,
Tell this soul with sorrow laden, if, within the
    distant Aidenn,
It shall clasp a sainted maiden, whom the
    angels name Lenore,
Clasp a fair and radiant maiden, whom the
    angels name Lenore!"
        Quoth the raven, "Nevermore!"

"Be that word our sign of parting, bird or
    fiend!" I shrieked, upstarting, —
"Get thee back into the tempest and the night's
    Plutonian shore!
Leave no black plume as a token of that lie thy
    soul hath spoken!
Leave my loneliness unbroken! — quit the bust
    above my door!
Take thy beak from out my heart, and take thy
    form from off my door!"
        Quoth the raven, "Nevermore!"

And the raven, never flitting, still is sitting,
    still is sitting
On the pallid bust of Pallas, just above my
    chamber door;

And his eyes have all the seeming of a demon
   that is dreaming,
And the lamplight o'er him streaming throws
   his shadow on the floor;
And my soul from out that shadow that lies
   floating on the floor
      Shall be lifted — *nevermore!*

Edgar Allan Poe

The Wreck of the Hesperus

It was the schooner Hesperus,
   That sailed the wintry sea;
And the skipper had taken his little daughter,
   To bear him company.

Blue were her eyes as the fairy-flax,
   Her cheeks like the dawn of day,
And her bosom white as the hawthorn buds,
   That ope in the month of May.

The skipper he stood beside the helm,
   His pipe was in his mouth,
And he watched how the veering flaw did blow
   The smoke now West, now South.

Then up spake an old Sailòr,
   Had sailed to the Spanish Main,

"I pray thee, put into yonder port,
    For I fear a hurricane.

"Last night, the moon had a golden ring,
    And to-night no moon we see!"
The skipper, he blew a whiff from his pipe,
    And a scornful laugh laughed he.

Colder and louder blew the wind,
    A gale from the Northeast,
The snow fell hissing in the brine,
    And the billows frothed like yeast.

Down came the storm, and smote amain
    The vessel in its strength;
She shuddered and paused, like a frighted
        steed,
    Then leaped her cable's length.

"Come hither! come hither! my little daughter,
    And do not tremble so;
For I can weather the roughest gale
    That ever wind did blow."

He wrapped her warm in his seaman's coat
    Against the stinging blast;
He cut a rope from a broken spar,
    And bound her to the mast.

"O father! I hear the church-bells ring,

Oh say, what may it be?''
'' 'Tis a fog-bell on a rock-bound coast!'' —
And he steered for the open sea.

''O father! I hear the sound of guns
   Oh say, what may it be?''
''Some ship in distress, that cannot live
   In such an angry sea!''

''O father! I see a gleaming light,
   Oh say, what may it be?''
But the father answered never a word,
   A frozen corpse was he.

Lashed to the helm, all stiff and stark,
   With his face turned to the skies,
The lantern gleamed through the gleaming
      snow
   On his fixed and glassy eyes.

Then the maiden clasped her hands and prayed
   That savèd she might be;
And she thought of Christ, who stilled the
      wave,
   On the Lake of Galilee.

And fast through the midnight dark and drear,
   Through the whistling sleet and snow,
Like a sheeted ghost, the vessel swept
   Tow'rds the reef of Norman's Woe.

And ever the fitful gusts between
  A sound came from the land;
It was the sound of the trampling surf
  On the rocks and the hard sea-sand.

The breakers were right beneath her bows,
  She drifted a dreary wreck,
And a whooping billow swept the crew
  Like icicles from her deck.

She struck where the white and fleecy waves
  Looked soft as carded wool,
But the cruel rocks, they gored her side
  Like the horns of an angry bull.

Her rattling shrouds, all sheathed in ice,
  With the masts went by the board;
Like a vessel of glass, she stove and sank,
  Ho! ho! the breakers roared!

At daybreak, on the bleak sea-beach,
  A fisherman stood aghast,
To see the form of a maiden fair,
  Lashed close to a drifting mast.

The salt sea was frozen on her breast,
  The salt tears in her eyes;
And he saw her hair, like the brown seaweed,
  On the billows fall and rise.

Such was the wreck of the Hesperus,
In the midnight and the snow!
Christ save us all from a death like this,
On the reef of Norman's Woe!
Henry Wadsworth Longfellow

Paul Revere's Ride

Listen, my children, and you shall hear
Of the midnight ride of Paul Revere,
On the eighteenth of April, in Seventy-five;
Hardly a man is now alive
Who remembers that famous day and year.

He said to his friend, "If the British march
By land or sea from the town tonight,
Hang a lantern aloft in the belfry arch
Of the North Church tower as a signal light, —
One, if by land, and two, if by sea;
And I on the opposite shore will be,
Ready to ride and spread the alarm
Through every Middlesex village and farm,
For the country folk to be up and to arm."

Then he said, "Good night!" and with muffled
   oar
Silently rowed to the Charlestown shore,
Just as the moon rose over the bay,

Where swinging wide at her moorings lay
The Somerset, British man-of-war;
A phantom ship, with each mast and spar
Across the moon like a prison bar,
And a huge black hulk, that was magnified
By its own reflection in the tide.

Meanwhile, his friend, through alley and
   street,
Wanders and watches with eager ears,
Till in the silence around him he hears
The muster of men at the barrack door,
The sound of arms, and the tramp of feet,
And the measured tread of the grenadiers,
Marching down to their boats on the shore.

Then he climbed the tower of the Old North
   Church,
By the wooden stairs, with stealthy tread,
To the belfry-chamber overhead,
And startled the pigeons from their perch
On the somber rafters, that round him made
Masses and moving shapes of shade, —
By the trembling ladder, steep and tall,
To the highest window in the wall,
Where he paused to listen and look down
A moment on the roofs of the town,
And the moonlight flowing over all.

Beneath, in the churchyard, lay the dead,

In their night-encampment on the hill,
Wrapped in silence so deep and still
That he could hear, like a sentinel's tread,
The watchful night-wind, as it went
Creeping along from tent to tent,
And seeming to whisper, "All is well!"
A moment only he feels the spell
Of the place and the hour, and the secret dread
Of the lonely belfry and the dead;
For suddenly all his thoughts are bent
On a shadowy something far away,
Where the river widens to meet the bay, —
A line of black that bends and floats
On the rising tide, like a bridge of boats.

Meanwhile, impatient to mount and ride,
Booted and spurred, with a heavy stride
On the opposite shore walked Paul Revere.
Now he patted his horse's side,
Now gazed at the landscape far and near,
Then, impetuous, stamped the earth,
And turned and tightened his saddle-girth;
But mostly he watched with eager search
The belfry-tower of the Old North Church,
As it rose above the graves on the hill,
Lonely and spectral and somber and still.
And lo! as he looks, on the belfry's height
A glimmer, and then a gleam of light!
He springs to the saddle, the bridle he turns,
But lingers and gazes, till full on his sight

A second lamp in the belfry burns!

A hurry of hoofs in a village street,
A shape in the moonlight, a bulk in the dark,
And beneath, from the pebbles, in passing, a
   spark
Struck out by a steed flying fearless and fleet;
That was all! And yet, through the gloom and
   the light
The fate of a nation was riding that night;
And the spark struck out by that steed in his
   flight,
Kindled the land into flame with its heat.

He has left the village and mounted the steep,
And beneath him, tranquil and broad and deep,
Is the Mystic, meeting the ocean tides;
And under the alders, that skirt its edge,
Now soft on the sand, now loud on the ledge,
Is heard the tramp of his steed as he rides.

It was twelve by the village clock
When he crossed the bridge into Medford
   town.
He heard the crowing of the cock,
And the barking of the farmer's dog,
And felt the damp of the river fog,
That rises after the sun goes down.

It was one by the village clock,

27

When he galloped into Lexington.
He saw the gilded weathercock
Swim in the moonlight as he passed,
And the meeting-house windows, blank and
   bare,
Gaze at him with a spectral glare,
As if they already stood aghast
At the bloody work they would look upon.

It was two by the village clock,
When he came to the bridge in Concord town.
He heard the bleating of the flock,
And the twitter of birds among the trees,
And felt the breath of the morning breeze
Blowing over the meadows brown.
And one was safe and asleep in his bed
Who at the bridge would be first to fall,
Who that day would be lying dead,
Pierced by a British musket-ball.

You know the rest. In the books you have
   read,
How the British Regulars fired and fled, —
How the farmers gave them ball for ball,
From behind each fence and farmyard wall,
Chasing the redcoats down the lane,
Then crossing the fields to emerge again
Under the trees at the turn of the road,
And only pausing to fire and load.
So through the night rode Paul Revere;

And so through the night went his cry of alarm
To every Middlesex village and farm, —
A cry of defiance, and not of fear,
A voice in the darkness, a knock at the door,
And a word that shall echo forevermore!
For, borne on the night-wind of the Past,
Through all our history, to the last,
In the hour of darkness and peril and need,
The people will waken and listen to hear
The hurrying hoofbeats of that steed,
And the midnight message of Paul Revere.

Henry Wadsworth Longfellow

My Last Duchess

Ferrara

That's my last Duchess painted on the wall,
Looking as if she were alive. I call
That piece a wonder, now: Fra Pandolf's hands
Worked busily a day, and there she stands.
Will't please you sit and look at her? I said
"Fra Pandolf" by design, for never read
Strangers like you that pictured countenance,
The depth and passion of its earnest glance,
But to myself they turned (since none puts by
The curtain I have drawn for you, but I)
And seemed as they would ask me, if they
    durst,

29

How such a glance came there; so, not the first
Are you to turn and ask thus. Sir, 'twas not
Her husband's presence only, called that spot
Of joy into the Duchess' cheek: perhaps
Fra Pandolf chanced to say, "Her mantle laps
Over my lady's wrist too much," or "Paint
Must never hope to reproduce the faint
Half-flush that dies along her throat": such
    stuff
Was courtesy, she thought, and cause enough
For calling up that spot of joy. She had
A heart — how shall I say? — too soon made
    glad,
Too easily impressed: she liked whate'er
She looked on, and her looks went
    everywhere.
Sir, 'twas all one! My favor at her breast,
The dropping of the daylight in the West,
The bough of cherries some officious fool
Broke in the orchard for her, the white mule
She rode with round the terrace — all and each
Would draw from her alike the approving
    speech,
Or blush, at least. She thanked men, — good!
    but thanked
Somehow — I know not how — as if she
    ranked
My gift of a nine-hundred-years-old name
With anybody's gift. Who'd stoop to blame
This sort of trifling? Even had you skill

In speech —(which I have not) — to make
  your will
Quite clear to such an one, and say, "Just this
Or that in you disgusts me; here you miss,
Or there exceed the mark" — and if she let
Herself be lessoned so, nor plainly set
Her wits to yours, forsooth, and made excuse,
— E'en then would be some stooping; and I
  choose
Never to stoop. Oh sir, she smiled, no doubt,
Whene'er I passed her; but who passed without
Much the same smile? This grew; I gave
  commands;
Then all smiles stopped together. There she
  stands
As if alive. Will't please you rise? We'll meet
The company below, then. I repeat,
The Count your master's known munificence
Is ample warrant that no just pretense
Of mine for dowry will be disallowed;
Though his fair daughter's self, as I avowed
At starting, is my object. Nay, we'll go
Together down, sir. Notice Neptune, though,
Taming a sea-horse, thought a rarity,
Which Claus of Innsbruck cast in bronze for
  me!

Robert Browning

The Deacon's Masterpiece,
or the Wonderful ''One-Hoss Shay''

A Logical Story

Have you heard of the wonderful one-hoss
   shay,
That was built in such a logical way
It ran a hundred years to a day,
And then, of a sudden, it — ah, but stay,
I'll tell you what happened without delay,
Scaring the parson into fits,
Frightening people out of their wits, —
Have you ever heard of that, I say?

Seventeen hundred and fifty-five.
Georgius Secundus was then alive, —
Snuffy old drone from the German hive.
That was the year when Lisbon-town
Saw the earth open and gulp her down,
And Braddock's army was done so brown,
Left without a scalp to its crown.
It was on the terrible Earthquake-day
That the Deacon finished the one-hoss shay.

Now in building of chaises, I tell you what,
There is always *somewhere* a weakest spot, —
In hub, tire, felloe, in spring or thill,
In panel, or crossbar, or floor, or sill,
In screw, bolt, thoroughbrace,— lurking still,

Find it somewhere you must and will, —
Above or below, or within or without, —
And that's the reason, beyond a doubt,
That a chaise *breaks down,* but doesn't *wear
out.*

But the Deacon swore (as Deacons do,
With an "I dew vum," or an "I tell *yeou,"*)
He would build one shay to beat the taown
'N' the keounty 'n' all the kentry raoun';
It should be so built that it *couldn'* break
    daown:
"Fur," said the Deacon, " 't's mighty plain
Thut the weakes' place mus' stan' the strain;
'N' the way t' fix it, uz I maintain,
    Is only jest
T' make that place uz strong uz the rest."

So the Deacon inquired of the village folk
Where he could find the strongest oak,
That couldn't be split nor bent nor broke, —
That was for spokes and floor and sills;
He sent for lancewood to make the thills;
The crossbars were ash, from the straightest
    trees,
The panels of white-wood, that cuts like
    cheese,
But lasts like iron for things like these;
The hubs of logs from the "Settler's
    ellum,"—

33

Last of its timber,— they couldn't sell 'em,
Never an axe had seen their chips,
And the wedges flew from between their lips,
Their blunt ends frizzled like celery-tips;
Step and prop-iron, bolt and screw,
Spring, tire, axle, and linchpin too,
Steel of the finest, bright and blue;
Thoroughbrace bison-skin, thick and wide;
Boot, top, dasher, from tough old hide
Found in the pit when the tanner died.
That was the way he "put her through."
"There!" said the Deacon, "naow she'll
    dew!"

Do! I tell you, I rather guess
She was a wonder, and nothing less!
Colts grew horses, beards turned gray,
Deacon and deaconess dropped away,
Children and grandchildren — where were
    they?
But there stood the stout old one-hoss shay
As fresh as on Lisbon-earthquake-day!

Eighteen hundred; — it came and found
The Deacon's masterpiece strong and sound.
Eighteen hundred increased by ten;
"Hahnsum kerridge" they called it then.
Eighteen hundred and twenty came; —
Running as usual; much the same.
Thirty and Forty at last arrive,

And then come Fifty, and Fifty-five.

Little of all we value here
Wakes on the morn of its hundredth year
Without both feeling and looking queer.
In fact, there's nothing that keeps its youth,
So far as I know, but a tree and truth.
(This is a moral that runs at large;
Take it. — You're welcome. — No extra
    charge.)

First of November, — the Earthquake-day, —
There are traces of age in the one-hoss shay.
A general flavor of mild decay,
But nothing local, as one may say.
There couldn't be, — for the Deacon's art
Had made it so like in every part
That there wasn't a chance for one to start.
For the wheels were just as strong as the thills,
And the floor was just as strong as the sills,
And the panels just as strong as the floor,
And the whipple-tree neither less nor more,
And the back-crossbar as strong as the fore,
And spring and axle and hub *encore*.
And yet, *as a whole,* it is past a doubt
In another hour it will be *worn out!*

First of November, Fifty-five!
This morning the parson takes a drive.
Now, small boys, get out of the way!

Here comes the wonderful one-hoss shay,
Drawn by a rat-railed, ewe-necked bay.
"Huddup!" said the parson. — off went they.

The parson was working his Sunday's text, —
Had got to *fifthly,* and stopped perplexed
At what the — Moses — was coming next.
All at once the horse stood still,
Close by the meet'n'-house on the hill.
First a shiver, and then a thrill,
Then something decidedly like a spill, —
And the parson was sitting upon a rock,
At half past nine by the meet'n'-house
    clock, —
Just the hour of the Earthquake shock!
What do you think the parson found,
When he got up and stared around?
The poor old chaise in a heap or mound,
As if it had been to the mill and ground!
You see, of course, if you're not a dunce,
How it went to pieces all at once, —
All at once, and nothing first, —
Just as bubbles do when they burst.

End of the wonderful one-hoss shay.
Logic is logic. That's all I say.
                                    Oliver Wendell Holmes

The Mills of the Gods

He was the slave of Ambition
And he vowed to the Gods above
To sell his soul to perdition
For Fortune, Fame, and Love.
"Three Wishes," he cried,
And the Devil replied:
"Fortune is a fickle one,
Often wooed but seldom won,
Ever changing like the sun;
Still, I think it can be done.
You have a friend, a rich one too;
Kill him! His wealth is willed to you."
Ambition fled. He paused awhile,
But, daunted by the Devil's smile,
He killed his friend to gain his aim,
Then bowed his head in grief and shame;
But the Devil cried, "It's all in the game.
You wanted Fortune, Love, and Fame,
And so, I came.
Three wishes through your life shall run,
Behold, I've given you Number One."

And the Gods on high, with a watchful eye,
Looked down on the ways of man,
With their hopes and fears through the weary
    years
Since the days of the world began.
And the man, he prayed, for the soul betrayed

Had breathed a parting call:
"Though the Mills of the Gods grind slowly,
Yet they grind exceeding small."

Urged by the spur of Ambition,
With the Devil still as his guide,
He now sought social position,
For wealth had brought him pride.
"Bring Fame," cried the man,
So the Devil began:
"Fame is but an accident,
Often sought but seldom sent,
Still, I think we're on the scent.

You know a genius gone insane;
Go steal the product of his brain.
The man obeyed, then cried, "Begone!
From crime to crime you lead me on,
To kill a friend whose smile was glad,
To rob a genius driven mad
Through want. Oh God! Am I that bad?"
But the Devil cried, "What luck you've had!
You're famous, lad!
Three wishes run your whole life through,
Behold, I've given you Number Two."
And the Gods looked down with an angry
    frown
Till Satan fled their scorn.
For the Devil may play with the common clay,
But genius is heaven-born.

And the man grew bold with his Fame and
    Gold,
And cried, "Well, after all,
The Mills of the Gods grind slowly,
If they ever grind at all."

Men, good or bad, are but human,
And he, like the rest, wanted love.
So the Devil soon brought him the woman
As fair as an angel above.
"I love you," he cried,
But the woman replied,
"Love is such an empty word,
Fancy fleeting like a bird,
You have Wealth and Fame, I've heard —
Those are things to be preferred."
He gave her both. The wealth she spent,
And then betrayed him, so Fame went.
But Love came not, in his despair;
She only smiled and left him there,
And he called her "The Woman Who Didn't
    Care,"
But the Devil cried, "You've had your share,
The game ends there.
Two of your wishes came through me,
But the Mighty Gods keep Number Three."

And the Gods grew stern as the Mills they
    turned,
That grind before they kill,

Till, staggering blind, with wandering mind,
And the glare of an imbecile,
From day to day he begs his way,
And whines his piteous call,
"The Mills of the Gods grind slowly,
Yet they grind exceeding small."

Unknown

Danny Deever

"What are the bugles blowin' for?" said Files-
on-Parade.
"To turn you out, to turn you out," the Color-
Sergeant said.
"What makes you look so white, so white?"
said Files-on-Parade.
"I'm dreadin' what I've got to watch," the
Color-Sergeant said.
For they're hangin' Danny Deever, you can
'ear the Dead March play,
The regiment's in 'ollow square — they're
hangin' him to-day;
They've taken of his buttons off an' cut his
stripes away,
An' they're hangin' Danny Deever in the
mornin'.

"What makes the rear-rank breathe so 'ard?"
said Files-on-Parade.

"It's bitter cold, it's bitter cold," the Color-
Sergeant said.
"What makes that front-rank man fall down?"
says Files-on-Parade.
"A touch o' sun, a touch o' sun," the Color-
Sergeant said.
They're hangin' Danny Deever, they are
marchin' of 'im round,
They 'ave 'alted Danny Deever by 'is coffin on
the ground;
An' 'e'll swing in 'arf a minute for a sneakin'
shootin' hound —
O they're hangin' Danny Deever in the mornin'!

" 'Is cot was right-'and cot to mine," said
Files-on-Parade.
" 'E's sleepin' out an' far to-night," the
Color-Sergeant said.
"I've drunk 'is beer a score o' times," said
Files-on-Parade.
" 'E's drinkin' bitter beer alone," the Color-
Sergeant said.
They are hangin' Danny Deever, you must
mark 'im to 'is place,
For 'e shot a comrade sleepin' — you must
look 'im in the face;
Nine 'undred of 'is county an' the regiment's
disgrace,
While they're hangin' Danny Deever in the
mornin'.

"What's that so black agin the sun?" said
 Files-on-Parade.
"It's Danny fightin' 'ard fur life," the Color-
 Sergeant said.
"What's that that whimpers over'ead?" said
 Files-on-Parade.
"It's Danny's soul that's passin' now," the
 Color-Sergeant said.
For they're done with Danny Deever, you can
 'ear the quickstep play,
The regiment's in column, an' they're marchin'
 us away;
Ho! the young recruits are shakin', an' they'll
 want their beer to-day,
After hangin' Danny Deever in the mornin'.

Rudyard Kipling

Mandalay

By the old Moulmein Pagoda, lookin' eastward
 to the sea,
There's a Burma girl a-settin', an' I know she
 thinks o' me;
For the wind is in the palm-trees, an' the
 temple bells they say:
"Come you back, you British soldier; come
 you back to Mandalay!"
Come you back to Mandalay,

Where the old Flotilla lay:
Can't you 'ear their paddles chunkin' from
   Rangoon to Mandalay?
On the road to Mandalay,
Where the flyin'-fishes play,
An' the dawn comes up like thunder outer
   China 'crost the Bay!

'Er petticut was yaller an' 'er little cap was
   green,
An' 'er name was Supi-yaw-let — jes' the
   same as Theebaw's Queen,
An' I seed her fust a-smokin' of a whackin'
   white cheroot,
An' a-wastin' Christian kisses on an 'eathen
   idol's foot:
   Bloomin' idol made o' mud —
   What they called the Great Gawd Budd —
   Plucky lot she cared for idols when I kissed
   'er where she stud!
   On the road to Mandalay —

When the mist was on the rice-fields an' the
   sun was droppin' slow
She'd git 'er little banjo an' she'd sing "*Kulla-
   lo-lo!*"
With 'er arm upon my shoulder an' her cheek
   agin my cheek
We useter watch the steamers an' the *hathis*
   pilin' teak.

Elephints a-pilin' teak
In the sludgy, squdgy creek,
Where the silence 'ung that 'eavy you was
  'arf afraid to speak!
On the road to Mandalay —

But that's all shove be'ind me — long ago an'
  fur away,
An' there ain't no 'busses runnin' from the
  Bank to Mandalay;
An' I'm learnin' 'ere in London what the ten-
  year sodger tells:
"If you've 'eard the East a-callin', why, you
  won't 'eed nothin' else."
  No! you won't 'eed nothin' else
  But them spicy garlic smells
  An' the sunshine an' the palm-trees an' the
  tinkly temple-bells!
On the road to Mandalay —

I am sick o' wastin' leather on these gritty
  pavin'-stones,
An' the blasted Henglish drizzle wakes the
  fever in my bones;
'Tho' I walks with fifty 'ousemaids outer
  Chelsea to the Strand,
An' they talks a lot o' lovin', but wot do they
  understand?
  Beefy face an' grubby 'and —
  Law! wot *do* they understand?

I've a neater, sweeter maiden in a cleaner,
    greener land!
On the road to Mandalay —

Ship me somewheres east of Suez where the
    best is like the worst,
Where there aren't no Ten Commandments,
    an' a man can raise a thirst:
For the temple-bells are callin', an' it's there
    that I would be —
By the old Moulmein Pagoda, lookin' lazy at
    the sea —
    On the road to Mandalay,
    Where the old Flotilla lay,
    With our sick beneath the awnings when we
        went to Mandalay!
    Oh, the road to Mandalay,
    Where the flyin'-fishes play,
    An' the dawn comes up like thunder outer
        China 'crost the Bay!

Rudyard Kipling

Gunga Din

You may talk o' gin and beer
When you're quartered safe out 'ere,
An' you're sent to penny-fights an' Aldershot
    it;
But when it comes to slaughter

You will do your work on water,
An' you'll lick the bloomin' boots of 'im that's
    got it.
Now in Injia's sunny clime,
Where I used to spend my time
A-servin' of 'Er Majesty the Queen,
Of all them blackfaced crew
The finest man I knew
Was our regimental bhisti, Gunga Din.
    He was "Din! Din! Din!
  "You limpin' lump o' brick-dust,
    Gunga Din!
    "Hi! Slippy *hitherao!*
    "Water, get it! *Panee lao!*[1]
  "You squidgy-nosed old idol, Gunga Din."

The uniform 'e wore
Was nothin' much before,
An' rather less than 'arf o' that be'ind,
For a piece o' twisty rag
An' a goatskin water-bag
Was all the field-equipment 'e could find.
When the sweatin' troop-train lay
In a sidin' through the day,
Where the 'eat would make your bloomin'
        eyebrows crawl,
We shouted "Harry by!"[2]
Till our throats were bricky-dry,

[1]Bring water swiftly. [2]O Brother.

46

Then we wopped 'im 'cause 'e couldn't serve
    us all.
    It was "Din! Din! Din!
  "You 'eathen, where the mischief 'ave you
    been?
    "You put some *juldee*[3] in it
    "Or I'll *marrow*[4] you this minute
"If you don't fill up my helmet, Gunga Din!"

'E would dot an' carry one
Till the longest day was done;
An' 'e didn't seem to know the use o' fear.
If we charged or broke or cut,
You could bet your bloomin' nut,
'E'd be waitin' fifty paces right flank rear.
With 'is mussick[5] on 'is back,
'E would skip with our attack,
An' watch us till the bugles made "Retire."
An' for all 'is dirty 'ide
'E was white, clear white, inside
When 'e went to tend the wounded under fire!
    It was "Din! Din! Din!"
  With the bullets kickin' dust-spots on the
    green.
    When the cartridges ran out,
    You could hear the front-ranks shout,
"Hi! ammunition-mules an' Gunga Din!"

[3]Be quick. [4]Hit you. [5]Water-skin.

47

I shan't forgit the night
When I dropped be'ind the fight
With a bullet where my belt-plate should 'a'
        been.
I was chokin' mad with thirst,
An' the man that spied me first
Was our good old grinnin', gruntin' Gunga
        Din.
'E lifted up my 'ead,
An' he plugged me where I bled,
An' 'e guv me 'arf-a-pint o' water green:
It was crawlin' and it stunk,
But of all the drinks I've drunk,
I'm gratefullest to one from Gunga Din.
        It was "Din! Din! Din!
    " 'Ere's a beggar with a bullet through 'is
            spleen;
        " 'E's chawin' up the ground,
        "An' 'e's kickin' all around:
    "For Gawd's sake git the water, Gunga
            Din!"

'E carried me away
To where a dooli lay,
An' a bullet come an' drilled the beggar clean.
'E put me safe inside,
An' just before 'e died,
"I 'ope you liked your drink," sez Gunga Din.
So I'll meet 'im later on
At the place where 'e is gone —

Where it's always double drill and no canteen;
'E'll be squattin' on the coals
Givin' drink to poor damned souls,
An' I'll get a swig in hell from Gunga Din!
　　Yes, Din! Din! Din!
　You Lazarushian-leather Gunga Din
　　Though I've belted you and flayed you,
　　By the livin' Gawd that made you,
　You're a better man than I am, Gunga Din!
　　　　　　　　　　Rudyard Kipling

Abdullah Bulbul Amir, or,
Ivan Petrofsky Skovar

The sons of the Prophet are valiant and bold,
　And quite unaccustomed to fear;
And the bravest of all was a man, so I'm told,
　Called Abdullah Bulbul Amir.

When they wanted a man to encourage the
　　van,
　Or harass the foe from the rear,
Storm fort or redoubt, they were sure to call
　　out
　For Abdullah Bulbul Amir.

There are heroes in plenty, and well known to
　　fame,
　In the legions that fight for the Czar;

But none of such fame as the man by the name
   Of Ivan Petrofsky Skovar.

He could imitate Irving, tell fortunes by cards,
   And play on the Spanish guitar;
In fact, quite the cream of the Muscovite
     guards,
   Was Ivan Petrofsky Skovar.

One day this bold Muscovite shouldered his
     gun,
   Put on his most cynical sneer,
And was walking downtown when he happened
     to run
   Into Abdullah Bulbul Amir.

"Young man," said Bulbul, "is existence so
     dull
   That you're anxious to end your career?
Then, infidel, know you have trod on the toe
   Of Abdullah Bulbul Amir.

"So take your last look at the sea, sky and
     brook,
   Make your latest report on the war;
For I mean to imply that you are going to die,
   O Ivan Petrofsky Skovar."

So this fierce man he took his trusty chibouk,
   And murmuring, "Allah Aklar!"

With murder intent he most savagely went
    For Ivan Petrofsky Skovar.

The Sultan rose up, the disturbance to quell,
    Likewise, give the victor a cheer.
He arrived just in time to bid hasty farewell
    To Abdullah Bulbul Amir.

A loud-sounding splash from the Danube was
      heard
    Resounding o'er meadows afar;
It came from the sack fitting close to the back
    Of Ivan Petrofsky Skovar.

There lieth a stone where the Danube doth roll,
    And on it in characters queer
Are "Stranger, when passing by, pray for the
    soul
    Of Abdullah Bulbul Amir."

A Muscovite maiden her vigil doth keep
    By the light of the pale northern star,
And the name she repeats every night in her
    sleep
    Is Ivan Petrofsky Skovar.

Unknown

The Face upon the Floor

'Twas a balmy summer evening, and a goodly
crowd was there.
Which well-nigh filled Joe's barroom on the
corner of the square,
And as songs and witty stories came through
the open door
A vagabond crept slowly in and posed upon
the floor.

"Where did it come from?" someone said:
"The wind has blown it in."
"What does it want?" another cried. "Some
whisky, rum or gin?"
"Here, Toby, seek him, if your stomach's
equal to the work —
I wouldn't touch him with a fork, he's as filthy
as a Turk."

This badinage the poor wretch took with stoical
good grace;
In fact, he smiled as though he thought he'd
struck the proper place.
"Come, boys, I know there's kindly hearts
among so good a crowd —
To be in such good company would make a
deacon proud.

"Give me a drink — that's what I want — I'm

out of funds, you know;
When I had cash to treat the gang, this hand
 was never slow.
What? You laugh as though you thought this
 pocket never held a sou;
I once was fixed as well, my boys, as anyone
 of you.

"There, thanks; that's braced me nicely; God
 bless you one and all;
Next time I pass this good saloon, I'll make
 another call.
Give you a song? No, I can't do that, my
 singing days are past;
My voice is cracked, my throat's worn out,
 and my lungs are going fast.

"Say! Give me another whisky, and I'll tell
 you what I'll do —
I'll tell you a funny story, and a fact, I
 promise, too.
That I was ever a decent man not one of you
 would think;
But I was, some four or five years back. Say,
 give me another drink.

"Fill her up, Joe, I want to put some life into
 my frame —
Such little drinks, to a bum like me, are
 miserably tame;

Five fingers — there, that's the scheme — and
  corking whisky, too.
Well, here's luck, boys; and, landlord, my best
  regards to you.

"You've treated me pretty kindly, and I'd like
  to tell you how
I came to be the dirty sot you see before you
  now.
As I told you, once I was a man, with muscle,
  frame and health,
And, but for a blunder, ought to have made
  considerable wealth.

"I was a painter — not one that daubed on
  bricks and wood
But an artist, and, for my age, was rated pretty
  good.
I worked hard at my canvas and was bidding
  fair to rise,
For gradually I saw the star of fame before my
  eyes.

"I made a picture, perhaps you've seen, 'tis
  called the 'Chase of Fame,'
It brought me fifteen hundred pounds and
  added to my name.
And then I met a woman — now comes the
  funny part —
With eyes that petrified my brain, and sunk

54

into my heart.

"Why don't you laugh? 'Tis funny that the
  vagabond you see
Could ever love a woman and expect her love
  for me;
But 'twas so, and for a month or two her
  smiles were freely given,
And when her loving lips touched mine it
  carried me to heaven.

"Did you ever see a woman for whom your
  soul you'd give,
With a form like the Milo Venus, too beautiful
  to live;
With eyes that would beat the Koh-i-noor, and
  a wealth of chestnut hair?
If so, 'twas she, for there never was another
  half so fair.

"I was working on a portrait, one afternoon in
  May,
Of a fair-haired boy, a friend of mine, who
  lived across the way,
And Madeline admired it, and, much to my
  surprise,
Said that she'd like to know the man that had
  such dreamy eyes.

"It didn't take long to know him, and before

55

the month had flown
My friend had stolen my darling, and I was
    left alone;
And, ere a year of misery had passed above
    my head,
The jewel I had treasured so had tarnished, and
    was dead.

"That's why I took to drink, boys. Why, I
    never saw you smile,
I thought you'd be amused, and laughing all
    the while.
Why, what's the matter, friend? There's a
    teardrop in your eye,
Come, laugh, like me; 'tis only babes and
    women that should cry.

"Say, boys, if you give me just another
    whisky, I'll be glad,
And I'll draw right here a picture of the face
    that drove me mad.
Give me that piece of chalk with which you
    mark the baseball score —
You shall see the lovely Madeline upon the
    barroom floor."

Another drink, and with chalk in hand the
    vagabond began
To sketch a face that well might buy the soul
    of any man.

Then, as he placed another lock upon the
    shapely head,
With a fearful shriek, he leaped and fell across
    the picture — dead.

H. Antoine D'Arcy

Casey at the Bat

It looked extremely rocky for the Mudville
    nine that day;
The score stood two to four, with but an inning
    left to play.
So, when Cooney died at second, and Burrows
    did the same,
A pallor wreathed the features of the patrons of
    the game.

A straggling few got up to go, leaving there
    the rest,
With that hope which springs eternal within the
    human breast.
For they thought: "If only Casey could get a
    whack at that,"
They'd put even money now, with Casey at the
    bat.

But Flynn preceded Casey, and likewise so did
    Blake,

And the former was a pudd'n, and the latter
   was a fake.
So on that stricken multitude a deathlike
   silence sat;
For there seemed but little chance of Casey's
   getting to the bat.

But Flynn let drive a "single," to the
   wonderment of all.
And the much-despised Blakey "tore the cover
   off the ball."
And when the dust had lifted, and they saw
   what had occurred,
There was Blakey safe at second, and Flynn
   a-huggin' third.

Then from the gladdened multitude went up a
   joyous yell —
It rumbled in the mountaintops, it rattled in the
   dell;
It struck upon the hillside and rebounded on
   the flat;
For Casey, mighty Casey, was advancing to
   the bat.

There was ease in Casey's manner as he
   stepped into his place,
There was pride in Casey's bearing and a smile
   on Casey's face;
And when responding to the cheers he lightly

doffed his hat,
No stranger in the crowd could doubt 'twas
    Casey at the bat.

Ten thousand eyes were on him as he rubbed
    his hands with dirt,
Five thousand tongues applauded when he
    wiped them on his shirt;
Then when the writhing pitcher ground the ball
    into his hip,
Defiance glanced in Casey's eye, a sneer
    curled Casey's lip.

And now the leather-covered sphere came
    hurtling through the air,
And Casey stood a-watching it in haughty
    grandeur there.
Close by the sturdy batsman the ball unheeded
    sped;
"That ain't my style," said Casey. "Strike
one," the umpire said.

From the benches, black with people, there
    went up a muffled roar,
Like the beating of the storm waves on the
    stern and distant shore.
"Kill him! kill the umpire!" shouted someone
    on the stand;
And it's likely they'd have killed him had not
    Casey raised his hand.

With a smile of Christian charity great Casey's
  visage shone;
He stilled the rising tumult, he made the game
  go on;
He signaled to the pitcher, and once more the
  spheroid flew;
But Casey still ignored it, and the umpire said,
  "Strike two."

"Fraud!" cried the maddened thousands, and
  the echo answered "Fraud!"
But one scornful look from Casey and the
  audience was awed;
They saw his face grow stern and cold, they
  saw his muscles strain,
And they knew that Casey wouldn't let the ball
  go by again.

The sneer is gone from Casey's lips, his teeth
  are clenched in hate,
He pounds with cruel vengeance his bat upon
  the plate;
And now the pitcher holds the ball, and now
  he lets it go,
And now the air is shattered by the force of
  Casey's blow.

Oh, somewhere in this favored land the sun is
  shining bright,

The band is playing somewhere, and
    somewhere hearts are light;
And somewhere men are laughing, and
    somewhere children shout,
But there is no joy in Mudville: Mighty Casey
    has struck out.

                    Ernest Lawrence Thayer

Miniver Cheevy

Miniver Cheevy, child of scorn,
    Grew lean while he assailed the seasons;
He wept that he was ever born,
    And he had reasons.

Miniver loved the days of old
    When swords were bright and steeds were
        prancing;
The vision of a warrior bold
    Would set him dancing.

Miniver sighed for what was not,
    And dreamed, and rested from his labors;
He dreamed of Thebes and Camelot,
    And Priam's neighbors.

Miniver mourned the ripe renown
    That made so many a name so fragrant;

He mourned Romance, now on the town,
  And Art, a vagrant.

Miniver loved the Medici,
  Albeit he had never seen one;
He would have sinned incessantly
  Could he have been one.

Miniver cursed the commonplace,
  And eyed a khaki suit with loathing;
He missed the medieval grace
  Of iron clothing.

Miniver scorned the gold he sought,
  But sore annoyed was he without it;
Miniver thought, and thought, and thought,
  And thought about it.

Miniver Cheevy, born too late,
  Scratched his head and kept on thinking;
Miniver coughed, and called it fate,
  And kept on drinking.
                Edwin Arlington Robinson

Richard Cory

Whenever Richard Cory went down town,
We people on the pavement looked at him:
He was a gentleman from sole to crown,

Clean favored, and imperially slim.

And he was always quietly arrayed,
And he was always human when he talked;
But still he fluttered pulses when he said,
"Good-morning," and he glittered when he
 walked.

And he was rich — yes, richer than a king —
And admirably schooled in every grace:
In fine, we thought that he was everything
To make us wish that we were in his place.

So on we worked, and waited for the light,
And went without the meat, and cursed the
 bread;
And Richard Cory, one calm summer night,
Went home and put a bullet through his head.
                    Edwin Arlington Robinson

The Shooting of Dan McGrew

A bunch of the boys were whooping it up in
 the Malamute saloon;
The kid that handles the music-box was hitting
 a jag-time tune;
Back of the bar, in a solo game, sat Dangerous
 Dan McGrew;

And watching his luck was his light-o'-love,
 the lady that's known as Lou.

When out of the night, which was fifty below,
 and into the din and the glare,
There stumbled a miner fresh from the creeks,
 dog-dirty, and loaded for bear.
He looked like a man with a foot in the grave
 and scarcely the strength of a louse,
Yet he tilted a poke of dust on the bar, and he
 called for drinks for the house.
There was none could place the stranger's face,
 though we searched ourselves for a clue;
But we drank his health, and the last to drink
 was Dangerous Dan McGrew.

There's men that somehow just grip your eyes,
 and hold them hard like a spell;
And such was he, and he looked to me like a
 man who had lived in hell;
With a face most hair, and the dreary stare of a
 dog whose day is done,
As he watered the green stuff in his glass, and
 the drops fell one by one.
Then I got to figgering who he was, and
 wondering what he'd do,
And I turned my head — and there watching
 him was the lady that's known as Lou.

His eyes went rubbering round the room, and

he seemed in a kind of daze,
Till at last that old piano fell in the way of his
wandering gaze.
The rag-time kid was having a drink; there was
no one else on the stool,
So the stranger stumbles across the room, and
flops down there like a fool.
In a buckskin shirt that was glazed with dirt he
sat, and I saw him sway;
Then he clutched the keys with his talon hands
— my God! but that man could play.

Were you ever out in the Great Alone, when
the moon was awful clear,
And the icy mountains hemmed you in with a
silence you most could *hear;*
With only the howl of a timber wolf, and you
camped there in the cold,
A half-dead thing in a stark, dead world, clean
mad for the muck called gold;
While high overhead, green, yellow and red,
the North Lights swept in bars? —
Then you've a hunch what the music meant
. . . hunger and night and the stars.

And hunger not of the belly kind, that's
banished with bacon and beans,
But the gnawing hunger of lonely men for a
home and all that it means;
For a fireside far from the cares that are, four

walls and a roof above;
But oh! so cramful of cosy joy, and crowned
  with a woman's love —
A woman dearer than all the world, and true as
  Heaven is true —
(God! how ghastly she looks through her rouge
  — the lady that's known as Lou.)

Then on a sudden the music changed, so soft
  that you scarce could hear;
But you felt that your life had been looted
  clean of all that it once held dear;
That someone had stolen the woman you loved;
  that her love was a devil's lie;
That your guts were gone, and the best for you
  was to crawl away and die.
'Twas the crowning cry of a heart's despair,
  and it thrilled you through and through —
"I guess I'll make it a spread misère," said
  Dangerous Dan McGrew.

The music almost died away . . . then it burst
  like a pent-up flood;
And it seemed to say, "Repay, repay," and
  my eyes were blind with blood.
The thought came back of ancient wrong, and
  it stung like a frozen lash.
And the lust awoke, to kill, to kill . . . then
  the music stopped with a crash,
And the stranger turned, and his eyes they

burned in a most peculiar way;
In a buckskin shirt that was glazed with dirt he
    sat, and I saw him sway;
Then his lips went in in a kind of grin, and he
    spoke, and his voice was calm,
And "Boys," says he, "you don't know me,
    and none of you care a damn;
But I want to state, and my words are straight,
    and I'll bet my poke they're true,
That one of you is a hound in hell . . . and
    that one is Dan McGrew."

Then I ducked my head, and the lights went
    out, and two guns blazed in the dark,
And a woman screamed, and the lights went
    up, and two men lay stiff and stark.
Pitched on his head, and pumped full of lead,
    was Dangerous Dan McGrew,
While the man from the creeks lay clutched to
    the breast of the lady that's known as Lou.
These are the simple facts of the case, and I
    guess I ought to know.
They say that the stranger was crazed with
    "hooch," and I'm not denying it's so.
I'm not so wise as the lawyer guys, but strictly
    between us two —
The woman that kissed him and — pinched his
    poke — was the lady that's known as Lou.

Robert W. Service

The Highwayman

Part I

The wind was a torrent of darkness among the
  gusty trees,
The moon was a ghostly galleon tossed upon
  cloudy seas,
The road was a ribbon of moonlight over the
  purple moor,
And the highwayman came riding —
    Riding — riding —
The highwayman came riding, up to the old
  inn-door.

He'd a French cocked-hat on his forehead, a
  bunch of lace at his chin.
A coat of the claret velvet, and breeches of
  brown doe-skin;
They fitted with never a wrinkle: his boots
  were up to the thigh!
And he rode with a jeweled twinkle,
    His pistol butts a-twinkle,
His rapier hilt a-twinkle, under the jeweled
  sky.

Over the cobbles he clattered and clashed in
  the dark inn-yard,
And he tapped with his whip on the shutters,
  but all was locked and barred;
He whistled a tune to the window, and who

68

should be waiting there
But the landlord's black-eyed daughter,
 Bess, the landlord's daughter,
Plaiting a dark red love-knot into her long
 black hair.

And dark in the dark old inn-yard a stable-
 wicket creaked
Where Tim the ostler listened; his face was
 white and peaked;
His eyes were hollows of madness, his hair
 like moldy hay,
But he loved the landlord's daughter,
 The landlord's red-lipped daughter,
Dumb as a dog he listened, and he heard the
 robber say —

"One kiss, my bonny sweetheart, I'm after a
 prize to-night,
But I shall be back with the yellow gold before
 the morning light;
Yet, if they press me sharply, and harry me
 through the day,
Then look for me by moonlight,
 Watch for me by moonlight,
I'll come to thee by moonlight, though hell
 should bar the way."

He rose upright in the stirrups; he scarce could
 reach her hand,

But she loosened her hair i' the casement! His
    face burnt like a brand
As the black cascade of perfume came
    tumbling over his breast;
And he kissed its waves in the moonlight,
      (Oh, sweet black waves in the moonlight!)
Then he tugged at his rein in the moonlight,
    and galloped away to the West.

Part II

He did not come in the dawning; he did not
    come at noon;
And out o' the tawny sunset, before the rise o'
    the moon,
When the road was a gipsy's ribbon, looping
    the purple moor,
A red-coat troop came marching —
      Marching — Marching —
King George's men came marching, up to the
    old inn-door.

They said no word to the landlord, they drank
    his ale instead,
But they gagged his daughter and bound her to
    the foot of her narrow bed;
Two of them knelt at her casement, with
    muskets at their side!
There was death at every window;
      And hell at one dark window;
For Bess could see, through her casement, the

70

road that *he* would ride.

They had tied her up to attention, with many a
  sniggering jest;
They had bound a musket beside her, with the
  barrel beneath her breast!
"Now keep good watch!" and they kissed her.
  She heard the dead man say —
Look for me by moonlight;
  Watch for me by moonlight;
I'll come to thee by moonlight, though hell
  should bar the way!

She twisted her hands behind her; but all the
  knots held good!
She writhed her hands till her fingers were wet
  with sweat or blood!
They stretched and strained in the darkness,
  and the hours crawled by like years,
Till, now, on the stroke of midnight,
  Cold, on the stroke of midnight,
The tip of one finger touched it! The trigger at
  least was hers!

The tip of one finger touched it; she strove no
  more for the rest!
Up, she stood up to attention, with the barrel
  beneath her breast,
She would not risk their hearing: she would not
  strive again;

71

For the road lay bare in the moonlight;
   Blank and bare in the moonlight;
And the blood of her veins in the moonlight
   throbbed to her love's refrain.

Tlot-tlot; tlot-tlot! Had they heard it? The
   horse-hoofs ringing clear;
Tlot-tlot, tlot-tlot, in the distance? Were they
   deaf that they did not hear?
Down the ribbon of moonlight, over the brow
   of the hill,
The highwayman came riding,
   Riding, riding!
The red-coats looked to their priming! She
   stood up, straight and still!

Tlot-tlot, in the frosty silence! *Tlot-tlot,* in the
   echoing night!
Nearer he came and nearer! Her face was like
   a light!
Her eyes grew wide for a moment; she drew
   one last deep breath,
Then her finger moved in the moonlight,
   Her musket shattered the moonlight,
Shattered her breast in the moonlight and
   warned him — with her death.

He turned; he spurred to the Westward; he did
   not know who stood
Bowed, with her head o'er the musket,

drenched with her own red blood!
Not till the dawn he heard it, his face grew
    gray to hear
How Bess, the landlord's daughter,
      The landlord's black-eyed daughter,
Had watched for her love in the moonlight,
    and died in the darkness there.

Back, he spurred like a madman, shrieking a
    curse to the sky,
With the white road smoking behind him, and
    his rapier brandished high!
Blood-red were his spurs in the golden noon;
    wine-red was his velvet coat,
When they shot him down on the highway,
      Down like a dog on the highway,
And he lay in his blood on the highway, with
    the bunch of lace at his throat.

. . . .

And still of a winter's night, they say, when
    the wind is in the trees,
When the moon is a ghostly galleon tossed
    upon cloudy seas,
When the road is a ribbon of moonlight over
    the purple moor,
A highwayman comes riding —
    Riding — riding —
A highwayman comes riding, up to the old inn-
    door.

Over the cobbles he clatters and clangs in the
*   dark inn-yard;*
And he taps with his whip on the shutters, but
*   all is locked and barred;*
He whistles a tune to the window, and who
*   should be waiting there*
But the landlord's black-eyed daughter,
*   Bess, the landlord's daughter,*
Plaiting a dark red love-knot into her long
*   black hair.*

*   Alfred Noyes*

Alumnus Football

Bill Jones had been the shining star upon his
    college team.
His tackling was ferocious and his bucking was
    a dream.
When husky Williams took the ball beneath his
    brawny arm
They had two extra men to ring the ambulance
    alarm.

Bill hit the line and ran the ends like some
    mad bull amuck.
The other team would shiver when they saw
    him start to buck.
And when some rival tackler tried to block his
    dashing pace,

On waking up, he'd ask, "Who drove that
   truck across my face?"

Bill had the speed — Bill had the weight —
   Bill never bucked in vain;
From goal to goal he whizzed along while
   fragments strewed the plain,
And there had been a standing bet, which no
   one tried to call,
That he could make his distance through a ten-
   foot granite wall.

When he wound up his college course each
   student's heart was sore.
They wept to think bull-throated Bill would
   sock the line no more.
Not so with William — in his dreams he saw
   the Field of Fame,
Where he would buck to glory in the swirl of
   Life's big game.

Sweet are the dreams of college life, before
   our faith is nicked —
The world is but a cherry tree that's waiting to
   be picked;
The world is but an open road — until we
   find, one day,
How far away the goal posts are that called us
   to the play.

So, with the sheepskin tucked beneath his arm
  in football style,
Bill put on steam and dashed into the thickest
  of the pile;
With eyes ablaze, he sprinted where the
  laureled highway led —
When Bill woke up his scalp hung loose and
  knot adorned his head.

He tried to run the ends of life but with rib-
  crushing toss
A rent-collector tackled him and threw him for
  a loss.
And when he switched his course again and
  dashed into the line
The massive Guard named Failure did a toddle
  on his spine.

Bill tried to punt out of the rut, but ere he
  turned the trick
Right Tackle Competition scuttled through and
  blocked the kick.
And when he tackled at Success in one long,
  vicious prod
The Fullback Disappointment steered his
  features in the sod.

Bill was no quitter, so he tried a buck in
  higher gear,

But Left Guard Envy broke it up and stood
   him on his ear.
Whereat he aimed a forward pass, but in a
   vicious bound
Big Center Greed slipped through a hole and
   slammed him to the ground.

But one day, when across the Field of Fame
   the goal seemed dim,
The wise old coach, Experience, came up and
   spoke to him.
"Oh boy," he said, "the main point now
   before you win your bout
Is keep on bucking Failure till you've worn the
   piker out!

"And, kid, cut out this fancy stuff — go in
   there, low and hard;
Just keep your eye upon the ball and plug on,
   yard by yard,
And more than all — when you are thrown or
   tumbled with a crack,
Don't sit there whining — hustle up and keep
   on coming back;

"Keep coming back with all you've got,
   without an alibi,
If Competition trips you up or lands upon your
   eye,
Until at last above the din you hear this

sentence spilled:
'We might as well let this bird through before
    we all get killed.'

"You'll find the road is long and rough, with
    soft spots far apart,
Where only those can make the grade who
    have the Uphill Heart.
And when they stop you with a thud or halt
    you with a crack,
Let Courage call the signals as you keep on
    coming back.

"Keep coming back, and though the world
    may romp across your spine,
Let every game's end find you still upon the
    battling line;
For when the One Great Scorer comes to mark
    against your name,
He writes — not that you won or lost — but
    how you played the Game."

Grantland Rice

Love and
Friendship

My Love Is Like to Ice

My love is like to ice, and I to fire:
How comes it then that this her cold so great
Is not dissolved through my so hot desire,
But harder grows the more I her entreat?
Or how comes it that my exceeding heat
Is not allayed by her heart-frozen cold,
But that I burn much more in boiling sweat,
And feel my flames augmented manifold?
What more miraculous thing may be told,
That fire, which all things melts, should harden
    ice,
And ice, which is congealed with senseless
    cold,
Should kindle fire by wonderful device?
Such is the power of love in gentle mind,
That it can alter all the course of kind.

Edmund Spenser

Now What Is Love

Now what is Love, I pray thee, tell?
It is that fountain and that well
Where pleasure and repentance dwell;

81

It is, perhaps, the sauncing bell
That tolls all into heaven or hell;
And this is Love, as I hear tell.

Yet what is Love, I prithee, say?
    It is a work on holiday,
    It is December matched with May,
    When lusty bloods in fresh array
    Hear ten months after of the play;
    And this is Love, as I hear say.

Yet what is Love, good shepherd, sain?
    It is a sunshine mixed with rain,
    It is a toothache or like pain,
    It is a game where none hath gain;
    The lass saith no, yet would full fain;
    And this is Love, as I hear sain.

Yet, shepherd, what is Love, I pray?
    It is a yes, it is a nay,
    A pretty kind of sporting fray,
    It is a thing will soon away.
    Then, nymphs, take vantage while ye may;
    And this is Love, as I hear say.

Yet what is Love, good shepherd, show?
    A thing that creeps, it cannot go,
    A prize that passeth to and fro,
    A thing for one, a thing for moe,

And he that proves shall find it so;
And shepherd, this is Love, I trow.
Walter Raleigh

Sonnet XVIII

Shall I compare thee to a Summer's day?
Thou art more lovely and more temperate:
Rough winds do shake the darling buds of
   May,
And Summer's lease hath all too short a date:
Sometime too hot the eye of heaven shines,
And often is his gold complexion dimmed;
And every fair from fair sometime declines,
By chance or nature's changing course
   untrimmed:
But thy eternal Summer shall not fade
Nor lose possession of that fair thou owest;
Nor shall Death brag thou wanderest in his
   shade,
When in eternal lines to time thou growest:
So long as men can breathe, or eyes can see,
So long lives this, and this gives life to thee.
William Shakespeare

Sonnet XXX

When to the sessions of sweet silent thought
I summon up remembrance of things past,
I sigh the lack of many a thing I sought,
And with old woes new wail my dear time's
    waste:
Then can I drown an eye, unused to flow,
For precious friends hid in death's dateless
    night,
And weep afresh love's long-since-cancell'd
    woe,
And moan th' expense of many a vanish'd
    sight:
Then can I grieve at grievances foregone,
And heavily from woe to woe tell o'er
The sad account of fore-bemoanèd moan,
Which I new pay as if not paid before.
    But if the while I think on thee, dear friend,
    All losses are restored and sorrows end.

William Shakespeare

Sonnet CIV

To me, fair friend, you never can be old;
For as you were when first your eye I eyed,
Such seems your beauty still. Three Winters
    cold

Have from the forests shook three Summers'
    pride;
Three beauteous Springs to yellow Autumn
    turn'd
In process of the seasons have I seen,
Three April perfumes in three hot Junes
    burn'd,
Since first I saw you fresh, which yet are
    green.
Ah! yet doth beauty, like a dial-hand,
Steal from his figure, and no pace perceived;
So your sweet hue, which methinks still doth
    stand,
Hath motion, and mine eye may be deceived:
  For fear of which, hear this, thou age
    unbred:
  Ere you were born was beauty's summer
    dead.

William Shakespeare

Sonnet CXVI

Let me not to the marriage of true minds
Admit impediments. Love is not love
Which alters when it alteration finds,
Or bends with the remover to remove:
O, no! it is an ever-fixèd mark,
That looks on tempests and is never shaken;
It is the star to every wand'ring bark,

Whose worth's unknown, although his height
    be taken.
Love's not Time's fool, though rosy lips and
    cheeks
Within his bending sickle's compass come;
Love alters not with his brief hours and weeks,
But bears it out even to the edge of doom: —
  If this be error and upon me proved,
  I never writ, nor no man ever loved.

                     William Shakespeare

The Passionate Shepherd to His Love

Come live with me and be my Love,
And we will all the pleasures prove
That hills and valleys, dales and fields,
Or woods or steepy mountain yields.

And we will sit upon the rocks,
And see the shepherds feed their flocks
By shallow rivers, to whose falls
Melodious birds sing madrigals.

And I will make thee beds of roses
And a thousand fragrant posies;
A cap of flowers, and a kirtle
Embroidered all with leaves of myrtle.

A gown made of the finest wool

Which from our pretty lambs we pull;
Fair-lined slippers for the cold,
With buckles of the purest gold.

A belt of straw and ivy-buds
With coral clasps and amber studs:
And if these pleasures may thee move,
Come live with me and be my Love.

The shepherd swains shall dance and sing
For thy delight each May morning:
If these delights thy mind may move,
Then live with me and be my Love.

Christopher Marlowe

The Good Morrow

I wonder, by my troth, what thou and I
Did, till we loved? were we not weaned till
    then?
But sucked on country pleasures, childishly?
Or snorted we in the Seven Sleepers' den?
'Twas so; but this, all pleasures fancies be;
If ever any beauty I did see,
Which I desired, and got, 'twas but a dream of
    thee.

And now good morrow to our waking souls,
Which watch not one another out of fear;

For love all love of other sights controls,
And makes one little room an everywhere.
Let sea-discoverers to new worlds have gone;
Let maps to other, worlds on worlds have
    shown;
Let us possess one world; each hath one, and is
    one.

My face in thine eye, thine in mine appears,
And true plain hearts do in the faces rest;
Where can we find two better hemispheres
Without sharp north, without declining west?
Whatever dies, was not mix'd equally;
If our two loves be one, or thou and I
Love so alike that none can slacken, none can
    die.

John Donne

The Ecstasy

Where, like a pillow on a bed,
    A pregnant bank swell'd up, to rest
The violet's reclining head,
    Sat we two, one another's best.
Our hands were firmly cemented
    By a fast balm, which thence did spring;
Our eye-beams twisted, and did thread
    Our eyes upon one double string;
So t' entergraft our hands, as yet

Was all the means to make us one;
And pictures in our eyes to get
    Was all our propagation.
As, 'twixt two equal armies, Fate
    Suspends uncertain victory,
Our souls (which to advance their state
    Were gone out) hung 'twixt her, and me.
And whilst our souls negotiate there,
    We like sepulchral statues lay;
All day, the same our postures were,
    And we said nothing, all the day.
If any, so by love refin'd,
    That he soul's language understood,
And by good love were grown all mind,
    Within convenient distance stood,
He (though he knew not which soul spake,
    Because both meant, both spake the same)
Might thence a new concoction take,
    And part far purer than he came.
This ecstasy doth unperplex
    (We said) and tell us what we love;
We see by this, it was not sex;
    We see, we saw not what did move:
But as all several souls contain
    Mixture of things, they know not what,
Love, these mix'd souls, doth mix again,
    And makes both one, each this and that.
A single violet transplant,
    The strength, the colour, and the size
(All which before was poor and scant)

Redoubles still, and multiplies.
When love with one another so
   Interanimates two souls,
That abler soul, which thence doth flow,
   Defects of loneliness controls.
We then, who are this new soul, know,
   Of what we are compos'd, and made,
For th'atomies of which we grow,
   Are souls, whom no change can invade.
But, O alas! so long, so far
   Our bodies why do we forbear?
They are ours, though not we; we are
   Th'intelligences, they the sphere.
We owe them thanks, because they thus
   Did us, to us, at first convey,
Yielded their senses' force to us,
   Nor are dross to us, but allay.
On man heaven's influence works not so,
   But that it first imprints the air;
For soul into the soul may flow,
   Though it to body first repair.
As our blood labours to beget
   Spirits, as like souls as it can,
Because such fingers need to knit
   That subtle knot, which makes us man;
So must pure lovers' souls descend
   T' affections and to faculties,
Which sense may reach and apprehend,
   Else a great prince in prison lies.
To'our bodies turn we then, that so

Weak men on love reveal'd may look;
   Love's mysteries in souls do grow,
   But yet the body is his book.
And if some lover, such as we,
   Have heard this dialogue of one,
Let him still mark us, he shall see
   Small change when we're to bodies gone.

John Donne

To Celia

Drink to me only with thine eyes,
   And I will pledge with mine;
Or leave a kiss but in the cup
   And I'll not look for wine.
The thirst that from the soul doth rise
   Doth ask a drink divine;
But might I of Jove's nectar sup
   I would not change for thine.

I sent thee late a rosy wreath,
   Not so much honoring thee
As giving it a hope that there
   It could not withered be;
But thou thereon didst only breathe
   And sent'st it back to me;
Since when it grows, and smells, I swear,
   Not of itself but thee!

Ben Jonson

To the Virgins

Gather ye rosebuds while ye may,
    Old Time is still a flying;
And this same flower that smiles to-day
    To-morrow will be dying.

The glorious lamp of Heaven, the sun,
    The higher he's a getting,
The sooner will his race be run,
    And nearer he's to setting.

The age is best which is the first,
    When youth and blood are warmer;
But being spent, the worse and worst
    Times still succeed the former.

Then be not coy, but use your time,
    And, while ye may, go marry;
For having lost but once your prime,
    You may forever tarry.

Robert Herrick

Whenas in Silks My Julia Goes

Whenas in silks my Julia goes,
Then, then, me thinks, how sweetly flowes
That liquefaction of her clothes.

Next, when I cast mine eyes and see
That brave vibration each way free,
O how that glittering taketh me!
                    Robert Herrick

The Constant Lover

Out upon it, I have loved
    Three whole days together!
And am like to love three more,
    If it prove fair weather.

Time shall moult away his wings
    Ere he shall discover
In the whole wide world again
    Such a constant lover.

But the spite on 't is, no praise
    Is due at all to me:
Love with me had made no stays,
    Had it any been but she.

Had it any been but she,
    And that very face,
There had been at least ere this
    A dozen dozen in her place.
                    Sir John Suckling

Why So Pale and Wan?

Why so pale and wan, fond lover?
  Prithee, why so pale?
Will, when looking well can't move her,
  Looking ill prevail?
Prithee, why so pale?

Why so dull and mute, young sinner?
  Prithee, why so mute?
Will, when speaking well can't win her,
  Saying nothing do 't?
Prithee, why so mute?

Quit, quit for shame! this will not move;
  This cannot take her.
If of herself she will not love,
  Nothing can make her:
  The devil take her!

Sir John Suckling

To Althea From Prison

When love with unconfinèd wings
  Hovers within my gates,
And my divine Althea brings
  To whisper at my grates;
When I lie tangled in her hair
  And fettered with her eye,

94

The birds that wanton in the air
  Know no such liberty.

When flowing cups pass swiftly round
  With no allaying Thames,
Our careless heads with roses crowned,
  Our hearts with loyal flames;
When thirsty grief in wine we steep,
  When healths and draughts go free,
Fishes that tipple in the deep
  Know no such liberty.

When, linnet-like confinèd,
  With shriller throat shall sing
The mercy, sweetness, majesty
  And glories of my King;
When I shall voice aloud how good
  He is, how great should be,
The enlargèd winds, that curl the flood,
  Know no such liberty.

Stone walls do not a prison make,
  Nor iron bars a cage;
Minds innocent and quiet take
  That for an hermitage:
If I have freedom in my love,
  And in my soul am free,
Angels alone, that soar above,
  Enjoy such liberty.

              Richard Lovelace

To His Coy Mistress

Had we but world enough, and time,
This coyness, Lady, were no crime.
We would sit down and think which way
To walk and pass our long love's day.
Thou by the Indian Ganges' side
Shouldst rubies find: I by the tide
Of Humber would complain. I would
love you ten years before the Flood,
And you should, if you please, refuse
Till the conversion of the Jews.
My vegetable love should grow
Vaster than empires, and more slow;
An hundred years should go to praise
Thine eyes and on thy forehead gaze;
Two hundred to adore each breast,
But thirty thousand to the rest;
An age at least to every part,
And the last age should show your heart.
For, Lady, you deserve this state,
Nor would I love at lower rate.
  But at my back I always hear
Time's winged chariot hurrying near:
And yonder all before us lie
Deserts of vast eternity.
Thy beauty shall no more be found,
Nor, in thy marble vault, shall sound
My echoing song: then worms shall try
That long preserved virginity,

And your quaint honor turn to dust,
And into ashes all my lust:
The grave's a fine and private place,
But none, I think, do there embrace.
  Now therefore, while the youthful hue
Sits on thy skin like morning dew,
And while thy willing soul transpires
At every pore with instant fires,
Now let us sport us while we may,
And now, like amorous birds of prey,
Rather at once our time devour
Than languish in his slow-chapt power.
Let us roll all our strength and all
Our sweetness up into one ball,
And tear our pleasures with rough strife
Through the iron gates of life:
Thus, though we cannot make our sun
Stand still, yet we will make him run.

Andrew Marvell

Woman

When lovely woman stoops to folly,
  And finds too late that men betray,
What charm can soothe her melancholy?
  What art can wash her tears away?

The only art her guilt to cover,
  To hide her shame from ev'ry eye,

To give repentance to her lover,
    And wring his bosom is — to die.
                    Oliver Goldsmith

My Luve

O my luve is like a red, red rose,
    That's newly sprung in June:
O my luve is like the melodie,
    That's sweetly played in tune.

As fair art thou, my bonie lass,
    So deep in luve am I;
And I will luve thee still, my dear,
    Till a' the seas gang dry.

Till a' the seas gang dry, my dear,
    And the rocks melt wi' the sun;
And I will luve thee still, my dear,
    While the sands o' life shall run.

And fare thee weel, my only luve!
    And fare thee weel a while!
And I will come again, my luve,
    Tho' it were ten thousand mile.
                    Robert Burns

Believe Me, If All Those
Endearing Young Charms

Believe me, if all those endearing young
    charms,
    Which I gaze on so fondly to-day,
Were to change by to-morrow, and fleet in my
    arms,
    Like fairy-gifts fading away,
Thou wouldst still be adored, as this moment
    thou art,
    Let thy loveliness fade as it will,
And around the dear ruin each wish of my
    heart
    Would entwine itself verdantly still.

It is not while beauty and youth are thine own,
    And thy cheeks unprofaned by a tear,
That the fervor and faith of a soul may be
    known,
    To which time will but make thee more
    dear!

No, the heart that has truly loved never
    forgets,
    But as truly loves on to the close,
As the sunflower turns to her god when he sets
    The same look which she turned when he
    rose!

Thomas Moore

Jenny Kissed Me

Jenny kissed me when we met,
   Jumping from the chair she sat in.
Time, you thief! who love to get
   Sweets into your list, put that in.
Say I'm weary, say I'm sad;
   Say that health and wealth have missed me;
Say I'm growing old, but add —
   Jenny kissed me!

Leigh Hunt

She Walks in Beauty

She walks in beauty like the night
   Of cloudless climes and starry skies;
And all that's best of dark and bright
   Meets in her aspect and her eyes:
Thus mellow'd to that tender light
   Which heaven to gaudy day denies.

One shade the more, one ray the less,
   Had half impair'd the nameless grace
Which waves in every raven tress,
   Or softly lightens o'er her face —
Where thoughts serenely sweet express
   How pure, how dear their dwelling-place.

And on that cheek, and o'er that brow,

So soft, so calm, yet eloquent,
The smiles that win, the tints that glow,
But tell of days in goodness spent,
A mind at peace with all below,
A heart whose love is innocent.

George Gordon, Lord Byron

When We Two Parted

When we two parted
In silence and tears,
Half broken-hearted,
To sever for years,
Pale grew thy cheek and cold,
Colder thy kiss;
Truly that hour foretold
Sorrow to this!

The dew of the morning
Sunk chill on my brow;
It felt like the warning
Of what I feel now.
Thy vows are all broken,
And light is thy fame:
I hear thy name spoken
And share in its shame.

They name thee before me,
A knell to mine ear;

A shudder comes o'er me —
Why wert thou so dear?
They know not I knew thee
Who knew thee too well:
Long, long shall I rue thee
Too deeply to tell.

In secret we met:
In silence I grieve
That thy heart could forget,
Thy spirit deceive.
If I should meet thee
After long years,
How should I greet thee? —
With silence and tears.
George Gordon, Lord Byron

The Flight of Love

When the lamp is shattered
The light in the dust lies dead —
When the cloud is scattered,
The rainbow's glory is shed.
When the lute is broken,
Sweet tones are remembered not;
When the lips have spoken,
Loved accents are soon forgot.

As music and splendor

Survive not the lamp and the lute,
The heart's echoes render
No song when the spirit is mute —
No song but sad dirges,
Like the wind through a ruined cell,
Or the mournful surges
That ring the dead seaman's knell.

When hearts have once mingled,
Love first leaves the well-built nest;
The weak one is singled
To endure what it once possessed.
O Love! who bewailest
The frailty of all things here,
Why choose you the frailest
For your cradle, your home, and your bier?

Its passions will rock thee
As the storms rock the ravens on high;
Bright reason will mock thee,
Like the sun from a wintry sky.
From thy nest every rafter
Will rot, and thine eagle home
Leave thee naked to laughter,
When leaves fall and cold winds come.

Percy Bysshe Shelley

Give All to Love

Give all to love;
Obey thy heart;
Friends, kindred, days,
Estate, good fame,
Plans, credit, and the Muse, —
Nothing refuse.

'Tis a brave master;
Let it have scope:
Follow it utterly,
Hope beyond hope:
High and more high
It dives into noon,
With wing unspent,
Untold intent;
But it is a god,
Knows its own path
And the outlets of the sky.

It was never for the mean;
It requireth courage stout.
Souls above doubt,
Valor unbending,
It will reward, —
They shall return
More than they were,
And ever ascending.

Leave all for love;
Yet, hear me, yet,
One word more thy heart behoved,
One pulse more of firm endeavor, —
Keep thee to-day,
To-morrow, forever,
Free as an Arab
Of thy beloved.

Cling with life to the maid;
but when the surprise,
First vague shadow of surmise,
Flits across her bosom young,
Of a joy apart from thee,
Free be she, fancy-free;
Nor thou detain her vesture's hem,
Nor the palest rose she flung
From her summer diadem.

Though thou loved her as thyself,
As a self of purer clay,
Though her parting dims the day,
Stealing grace from all alive;
Heartily know,
When half-gods go,
The gods arrive.

Ralph Waldo Emerson

How Do I Love Thee?

How do I love thee? Let me count the ways.
I love thee to the depth and breadth and height
My soul can reach, when feeling out of sight
For the ends of Being and ideal Grace.
I love thee to the level of every day's
Most quiet need, by sun and candlelight.
I love thee freely, as men strive for Right;
I love thee purely, as they turn from Praise.
I love thee with the passion put to use
In my old griefs, and with my childhood's
    faith.
I love thee with a love I seemed to lose
With my lost saints — I love thee with the
    breath,
Smiles, tears, of all my life! — and, if God
    choose,
I shall but love thee better after death.
             Elizabeth Barrett Browning

To Helen

Helen, thy beauty is to me
   Like those Nicaean barks of yore,
That gently, o'er a perfumed sea,
   The weary, wayworn wanderer bore
   To his own native shore.

On desperate seas long wont to roam,
  Thy hyacinth hair, thy classic face,
Thy Naiad airs, have brought me home
  To the glory that was Greece
  And the grandeur that was Rome.

Lo! in yon brilliant window-niche
  How statue-like I see thee stand,
The agate lamp within thy hand!
  Ah, Psyche, from the regions which
  Are Holy Land!

Edgar Allan Poe

Longing

Come to me in my dreams, and then
By day I shall be well again!
For then the night will more than pay
The hopeless longing of the day.

Come, as thou cam'st a thousand times,
A messenger from radiant climes,
And smile on thy new world, and be
As kind to others as to me!

Or, as thou never cam'st in sooth,
Come now, and let me dream it truth;
And part my hair, and kiss my brow,
And say: *My love! why sufferest thou?*

Come to me in my dreams, and then
By day I shall be well again!
For then the night will more than pay
The hopeless longing of the day.

Matthew Arnold

Sudden Light

I have been here before,
    But when or how I cannot tell.
I know the grass beyond the door,
    The sweet keen smell,
The sighing sound, the lights around the shore.

You have been mine before —
    How long ago I may not know;
But just when at that swallow's soar
    Your neck turned so,
Some veil did fall — I knew it all of yore.

Has this been thus before?
    And shall not thus time's eddying flight
Still with our lives our love restore
    In death's despite,
And day and night yield one delight once
      more?

Dante Gabriel Rossetti

Remember

Remember me when I am gone away,
Gone far away into the silent land;
When you can no more hold me by the hand,
Nor I half turn to go, yet turning stay.
Remember me when no more, day by day,
You tell me of our future that you planned:
Only remember me; you understand
It will be late to counsel then or pray.
Yet if you should forget me for a while
And afterwards remember, do not grieve:
For if the darkness and corruption leave
A vestige of the thoughts that once I had,
Better by far you should forget and smile
Than that you should remember and be sad.

Christina Georgina Rossetti

I Had No Time to Hate

I had no time to Hate —
Because
The Grave would hinder Me —
And Life was not so
Ample I
Could finish — Enmity —

Nor had I time to Love —
But since

Some Industry must be—
The little Toil of Love —
I thought
Be large enough for Me —
                    Emily Dickinson

An Old Sweetheart of Mine

An old sweetheart of mine! — Is this her
    presence here with me,
Or but a vain creation of a lover's memory?
A fair, illusive vision that would vanish into
    air,
Dared I even touch the silence with the
    whisper of a prayer?

Nay, let me then believe in all the blended
    false and true —
The semblance of the old love and the
    substance of the *new,* —
The *then* of changeless sunny days — the *now*
    of shower and shine —
But Love forever smiling — as that old
    sweetheart of mine.

This ever restful sense of *home* though shouts
    ring in the hall, —
The easy chair — the old book-shelves and

110

prints along the wall;
The rare *Habanas* in their box, or gaunt
    churchwarden-stem
That often wags, above the jar, derisively at
    them.

As one who cons at evening o'er an album, all
    alone,
And muses on the faces of the friends that he
    has known,
So I turn the leaves of Fancy, till, in a
    shadowy design,
I find the smiling features of an old sweetheart
    of mine.

I give my *treasures* to her — all, — my pencil
    — blue and red; —
And, if little girls played marbles, *mine* should
    all be *hers,* instead!
But *she* gave me her *photograph,* and printed
    ''Ever Thine''
Across the back — in blue and red — that old
    sweetheart of mine!

And again I feel the pressure of her slender
    little hand,
As we used to talk together of the future we
    had planned, —
When I should be a poet, and with nothing else
    to do

But write the tender verses that she set the
  music to . . .

Then we should live together in a cozy little
  cot
Hid in a nest of roses, with a fairy garden
  spot,
Where the vines were ever fruited, and the
  weather ever fine,
And the birds were ever singing for that old
  sweetheart of mine.

When I should be her lover forever and a day,
And she my faithful sweetheart till the golden
  hair was gray;
And we should be so happy that when either's
  lips were dumb
They would not smile in Heaven till the other's
  kiss had come.

But, ah! my dream is broken by a step upon
  the stair,
And the door is softly opened, and — my wife
  is standing there;
Yet with eagerness and rapture all my vision I
  resign, —
To greet the *living* presence of that old
  sweetheart of mine.

James Whitcomb Riley

A Mile with Me

O who will walk a mile with me
   Along life's merry way?
A comrade blithe and full of glee,
Who dares to laugh out loud and free,
And let his frolic fancy play,
Like a happy child, through the flowers gay
That fill the field and fringe the way
   Where he walks a mile with me.

And who will walk a mile with me
   Along life's weary way?
A friend whose heart has eyes to see
The stars shine out o'er the darkening lea,
And the quiet rest at the end o' the day, —
A friend who knows, and dares to say,
The brave, sweet words that cheer the way
   Where he walks a mile with me.

With such a comrade, such a friend,
I fain would walk till journey's end,
Through summer sunshine, winter rain,
And then? — Farewell, we shall meet again!
Henry Van Dyke

When I Was One-and-Twenty

When I was one-and-twenty
  I heard a wise man say,
"Give crowns and pounds and guineas
  But not your heart away;
Give pearls away and rubies
  But keep your fancy free."
But I was one-and-twenty,
  No use to talk to me.

When I was one-and-twenty
  I heard him say again,
"The heart out of the bosom
  Was never given in vain;
'Tis paid with sighs a plenty
  And sold for endless rue."
And I am two-and-twenty,
  And oh, 'tis true, 'tis true.

A. E. Housman

Non Sum Qualis Eram
Bonae Sub Regno Cynarae

Last night, ah, yesternight, betwixt her lips and
  mine
There fell thy shadow, Cynara! Thy breath was
  shed

Upon my soul between the kisses and the
   wine;
And I was desolate and sick of an old
passion —
Yea, I was desolate and bowed my head.
I have been faithful to thee, Cynara! — In my
   fashion.

All night upon mine heart I felt her warm heart
   beat,
Night-long within mine arms in love and sleep
   she lay;
Surely the kisses of her bought red mouth were
   sweet;
But I was desolate and sick of an old passion,
When I woke and found the dawn was gray:
I have been faithful to thee, Cynara! — In my
   fashion.

I have forgot much, Cynara! Gone with the
   wind,
Flung roses, roses riotously with the throng,
Dancing, to put thy pale, lost lilies out of
   mind;
But I was desolate and sick of an old
   passion —
Yea, all the time, because the dance was long:
   I have been faithful to thee, Cynara! — In my
   fashion.

I cried for madder music and for stronger
   wine,
but when the feast is finished and the lamps
   expire,
Then falls thy shadow, Cynara! the night is
   thine;
And I am desolate and sick of an old passion,
Yea, hungry for the lips of my desire:
I have been faithful to thee, Cynara! — In my
   fashion.

Ernest Dowson

To a Friend

I ask but one thing of you, only one,
   That always you will be my dream of you;
   That never shall I wake to find untrue
All this I have believed and rested on,
Forever vanished, like a vision gone
   Out into the night. Alas how few
   There are who strike in us a chord we knew
Existed, but so seldom heard its tone
   We tremble at the half-forgotten sound.
The world is full of rude awakenings
   And heaven-born castles shattered to the
      ground,
Yet still our human longing vainly clings
   To a belief in beauty through all wrongs.

O stay your hand, and leave my heart its
   songs!

Amy Lowell

The Great Lover

I have been so great a lover: filled my days
So proudly with the splendour of Love's
   praise,
The pain, the calm, and the astonishment,
Desire illimitable, and still content,
And all dear names men use, to cheat despair,
For the perplexed and viewless streams that
   bear
Our hearts at random down the dark of life.
Now, ere the unthinking silence on that strife
Steals down, I would cheat drowsy Death so
   far,
My night shall be remembered for a star
That outshone all the suns of all men's days.
Shall I not crown them with immortal praise
Whom I have loved, who have given me,
   dared with me
High secrets, and in darkness knelt to see
The inenarrable godhead of delight?
Love is a flame; — we have beaconed the
   world's night.
A city: — and we have built it, these and I.
An emperor: — we have taught the world to

die.
So, for their sakes I loved, ere I go hence,
And the high cause of Love's magnificence,
And to keep loyalties young, I'll write those
    names
Golden for ever, eagles, crying flames,
And set them as a banner, that men may know,
To dare the generations, burn, and blow
Out on the wind of Time, shining and
    streaming. . . .

These I have loved:
          White plates and cups, clean-gleaming,
Ringed with blue lines; and feathery, faery
    dust,
Wet roofs, beneath the lamp-light; the strong
    crust
Of friendly bread; and many-tasting food;
Rainbows; and the blue bitter smoke of wood;
And radiant raindrops couching in cool
    flowers;
And flowers themselves, that sway through
    sunny hours,
Dreaming of moths that drink them under the
    moon;
Then, the cool kindliness of sheets, that soon
Smooth away trouble; and the rough male kiss
Of blankets; grainy wood; live hair that is
Shining and free; blue-massing clouds; the
    keen

Unpassioned beauty of a great machine;
The benison of hot water; furs to touch;
The good smell of old clothes; and other
    such —
The comfortable smell of friendly fingers,
Hair's fragrance, and the musty reek that
    lingers
About dead leaves and last year's ferns. . . .
                        Dear names,
And thousand others throng to me! Royal
    flames;
Sweet water's dimpling laugh from tap or
    spring;
Holes in the ground; and voices that do sing:
Voices in laughter, too; and body's pain,
Soon turned to peace; and the deep-panting
    train;
Firm sands; the little dulling edge of foam
That browns and dwindles as the wave goes
    home;
And washen stones, gay for an hour; the cold
Graveness of iron; moist black earthen mould;
Sleep; and high places; footprints in the dew;
And oaks; and brown horse-chestnuts, glossy-
    new;
And new-peeled sticks; and shining pools on
    grass; —
All these have been my loves. And these shall
    pass.
Whatever passes not, in the great hour,

Nor all my passion, all my prayers, have
    power
To hold them with me through the gate of
    Death.
They'll play deserter, turn with traitor breath,
Break the high bond we made, and sell Love's
    trust
And sacramental covenant to the dust.

— Oh, never a doubt but, somewhere, I shall
    wake,
And give what's left of love again, and make
New friends, now strangers. . . .
                        But the best I've known,
Stays here, and changes, breaks; grows old, is
    blown
About the winds of the world, and fades from
    brains
Of living men and dies.
                        Nothing remains.

O dear my loves, O faithless, once again
This one last gift I give: that after men
Shall know, and later lovers, far-removed
Praise you, "All these were lovely"; say,
    "He loved."

                                    Rupert Brooke

You Kissed Me

You kissed me! My head drooped low on your
    breast
With a feeling of shelter and infinite rest,
While the holy emotions my tongue dared not
    speak,
Flashed up as in flame, from my heart to my
    cheek,
Your arms held me fast; oh! your arms were so
    bold —
Heart beat against heart in their passionate fold.
Your glances seemed drawing my soul through
    mine eyes,
As the sun draws the mist from the sea to the
    skies.
Your lips clung to mine till I prayed in my
    bliss
They might never unclasp from the rapturous
    kiss.

You kissed me! My heart, my breath and my
    will
In delirious joy for a moment stood still.
Life had for me then no temptations, no
    charms,
No visions of rapture outside of your arms;
And were I this instant an angel possessed
Of the peace and the joy that belong to the
    blest,

I would fling my white robes unrepiningly
   down,
I would tear from my forehead its beautiful
   crown,
To nestle once more in that haven of rest —
Your lips upon mine, my head on your breast.

You kissed me! My soul in a bliss so divine
Reeled and swooned like a drunkard when
   foolish with wine,
And I thought 'twere delicious to die there, if
   death
Would but come while my lips were yet moist
   with your breath;
While your arms clasped me round in that
   blissful embrace,
While your eyes melt in mine could e'en death
   e'er efface —
Oh, these are the questions I ask day and
   night:
Must my lips taste no more such exquisite
   delight?
Would you wish that your breast were my
   shelter as then?
And if you were here, would you kiss me
   again?

Josephine Slocum Hunt

122

Ad Finem

On the white throat of the useless passion
   That scorched my soul with its burning
      breath
I clutched my fingers in murderous fashion,
   And gathered them close in a grip of death;
For why should I fan, or feed with fuel,
   A love that showed me but blank despair?
So my hold was firm, and my grasp was
      cruel —
   I meant to strangle it then and there!

I thought it was dead. But with no warning,
   It rose from its grave last night, and came
And stood by my bed till the early morning,
   And over and over it spoke your name
Its throat was red where my hands had held it;
   It burned my brow with its scorching breath;
And I said, the moment my eyes beheld it,
   "A love like this can know no death."

For just one kiss that your lips have given
   In the lost and beautiful past to me,
I would gladly barter my hopes of Heaven
   And all the bliss of Eternity.
For never a joy are the angels keeping,
   To lay at my feet in Paradise,
Like that of into your strong arms creeping,
   And looking into your love-lit eyes.

I know, in the way that sins are reckoned,
    This thought is a sin of the deepest dye;
But I know, too, if an angel beckoned,
    Standing close by the Throne on High,
And you, adown by the gates infernal,
    Should open your loving arms and smile,
I would turn my back on things supernal,
    To lie on your breast a little while.

To know for an hour you were mine
        completely —
    Mine in body and soul, my own —
I would bear unending tortures sweetly,
    With not a murmur and not a moan.
A lighter sin or a lesser error
    Might change through hope or fear divine;
But there is no fear, and hell has no terror,
    To change or alter a love like mine.
                    Ella Wheeler Wilcox

I Love You

I love your lips when they're wet with wine
    And red with a wild desire;
I love your eyes when the lovelight lies
    Lit with a passionate fire.
I love your arms when the warm white flesh
    Touches mine in a fond embrace;

I love your hair when the strands enmesh
  Your kisses against my face.

Not for me the cold, calm kiss
  Of a virgin's bloodless love;
Not for me the saint's white bliss,
  Nor the heart of a spotless dove.
But give me the love that so freely gives
  And laughs at the whole world's blame,
With your body so young and warm in my
      arms,
  It sets my poor heart aflame.

So kiss me sweet with your warm wet mouth,
  Still fragrant with ruby wine,
And say with a fervor born of the South
  That your body and soul are mine.
Clasp me close in your warm young arms,
  While the pale stars shine above,
And we'll live our whole young lives away
  In the joys of a living love.
                    Ella Wheeler Wilcox

Love Is Not All: It Is Not
Meat Nor Drink

Love is not all: it is not meat nor drink
Nor slumber nor a roof against the rain;
Nor yet a floating spar to men that sink

And rise and sink and rise and sink again;
Love cannot fill the thickened lung with
   breath,
Nor clean the blood, nor set the fractured bone;
Yet many a man is making friends with death
Even as I speak, for lack of love alone.
It well may be that in a difficult hour,
Pinned down by pain and moaning for release,
Or nagged by want past resolution's power,
I might be driven to sell your love for peace,
Or trade the memory of this night for food.
It well may be. I do not think I would.

Edna St. Vincent Millay

Nature and
the Seasons

On the Death of a Favorite Cat, Drowned in a Tub of Gold Fishes

'Twas on a lofty vase's side,
Where China's gayest art had dyed
    The azure flowers that blow;
Demurest of the tabby kind,
The pensive Selima, reclined,
    Gazed on the lake below.

Her conscious tail her joy declared;
The fair round face, the snowy beard,
    The velvet of her paws,
Her coat, that with the tortoise vies,
Her ears of jet, and emerald eyes,
    She saw; and purred applause.

Still had she gazed, but 'midst the tide
Two angel forms were seen to glide,
    The Genii of the stream:
Their scaly armor's Tyrian hue
Through richest purple to the view
    Betrayed a golden gleam.

The hapless Nymph with wonder saw:
A whisker first and then a claw,

With many an ardent wish,
She stretched, in vain, to reach the prize.
What female heart can gold despise?
    What Cat's averse to fish?

Presumptuous Maid! with looks intent
Again she stretched, again she bent,
    Nor knew the gulf between.
(Malignant Fate sat by, and smiled.)
The slippery verge her feet beguiled,
    She tumbled headlong in.

Eight times emerging from the flood
She mewed to every watery god,
    Some speedy aid to send.
No Dolphin came, no Nereid stirred:
No cruel Tom nor Susan heard, —
    A Favorite has no friend!

From hence, ye Beauties, undeceived,
Know, one false step is ne'er retrieved,
    And be with caution bold.
Not all that tempts your wandering eyes
And heedless hearts, is lawful prize;
    Nor all that glisters, gold.

Thomas Gray

The Tiger

Tiger! Tiger! burning bright,
In the forests of the night,
What immortal hand or eye
Could frame thy fearful symmetry?

In what distant deeps or skies
Burnt the fire of thine eyes?
On what wings dare he aspire?
What the hand dare seize the fire?

And what shoulder, and what art,
Could twist the sinews of thy heart?
And when thy heart began to beat,
What dread hand and what dread feet?

What the hammer? what the chain?
In what furnace was thy brain?
What the anvil? what dread grasp
Dare its deadly terrors clasp?

When the stars threw down their spears,
And watered heaven with their tears,
Did He smile His work to see?
Did He who made the Lamb, make thee?

Tiger! Tiger! burning bright,
In the forests of the night,
What immortal hand or eye
Dare frame thy fearful symmetry?

William Blake

To the Evening Star

Thou fair-hair'd angel of the evening,
Now, whilst the sun rests on the mountains,
  light
Thy bright torch of love; thy radiant crown
Put on, and smile upon our evening bed!
Smile on our loves, and, while thou drawest
  the
Blue curtains of the sky, scatter thy silver dew
On every flower that shuts its sweet eyes
In timely sleep. Let thy west wind sleep on
The lake; speak silence with thy glimmering
  eyes,
And wash the dusk with silver. Soon, full soon,
Dost thou withdraw; then the wolf rages wide,
And the lion glares thro' the dun forest:
The fleeces of our flocks are cover'd with
Thy sacred dew: protect them with thine
  influence.

William Blake

The Rainbow

My heart leaps up when I behold
  A Rainbow in the sky:
So was it when my life began;
So is it now I am a Man;

So be it when I shall grow old,
   Or let me die!
The Child is Father of the Man;
And I could wish my days to be
Bound each to each by natural piety.
               William Wordsworth

Lines Written in Early Spring

I heard a thousand blended notes,
While in a grove I sat reclined,
In that sweet mood when pleasant thoughts
Bring sad thoughts to the mind.

To her fair works did Nature link
The human soul that through me ran;
And much it grieved my heart to think
What Man has made of Man.

Through primrose tufts, in that sweet bower,
The periwinkle trailed its wreaths;
And 'tis my faith that every flower
Enjoys the air it breathes.

The birds around me hopped and played,
Their thoughts I cannot measure, —
But the least motion which they made
It seemed a thrill of pleasure.

The budding twigs spread out their fan
To catch the breezy air;
And I must think, do all I can,
That there was pleasure there.

If this belief from heaven be sent,
If such be Nature's holy plan,
Have I not reason to lament
What Man has made of Man?

William Wordsworth

Daffodils

I wandered lonely as a cloud
    That floats on high o'er vales and hills,
When all at once I saw a crowd, —
    A host of golden daffodils
Beside the lake, beneath the trees,
Fluttering and dancing in the breeze.

Continuous as the stars that shine
    And twinkle on the Milky Way,
They stretched in never-ending line
    Along the margin of a bay:
Ten thousand saw I, at a glance,
Tossing their heads in sprightly dance.

The waves beside them danced, but they
    Outdid the sparkling waves in glee;

A poet could not but be gay
   In such a jocund company;
I gazed — and gazed — but little thought
What wealth the show to me had brought.

For oft, when on my couch I lie,
   In vacant or in pensive mood,
They flash upon that inward eye
   Which is the bliss of solitude;
And then my heart with pleasure fills,
And dances with the daffodils.
              William Wordsworth

To a Sky-Lark

Up with me! up with me into the clouds!
   For thy song, Lark, is strong;
Up with me, up with me into the clouds!
   Singing, singing,
With clouds and sky about thee ringing,
   Lift me, guide me till I find
That spot which seems so to thy mind.

I have walked through wildernesses dreary,
And to-day my heart is weary;
Had I now the wings of a Faery
Up to thee would I fly.
There is madness about thee, and joy divine
In that song of thine;

Lift me, guide me, high and high
To thy banqueting-place in the sky!

Joyous as morning,
Thou art laughing and scorning;
Thou hast a nest for thy love and thy rest,
And, though little troubled with sloth,
Drunken Lark! thou wouldst be loath
To be such a traveler as I.
Happy, happy Liver,
With a soul as strong as a mountain river
Pouring out praise to the almighty Giver,
Joy and jollity be with us both!

Alas! my journey, rugged and uneven,
Through prickly moors, or dusty ways must
    wind;
But hearing thee, or others of thy kind,
    As full of gladness and as free of heaven,
I, with my fate contented, will plod on,
And hope for higher raptures, when life's day
    is done.

William Wordsworth

Ode to the West Wind

I

O wild West Wind, thou breath of Autumn's
    being,

Thou from whose unseen presence the leaves
    dead
Are driven, like ghosts from an enchanter
    fleeing,

    Yellow, and black, and pale, and hectic red,
Pestilence-stricken multitudes! O thou
    Who chariotest to their dark wintry bed

The winged seeds, where they lie cold and
    low,
    Each like a corpse within its grave, until
Thine azure sister of the Spring shall blow

    Her clarion o'er the dreaming earth, and fill
(Driving sweet buds like flocks to feed in air)
    With living hues and odors plain and hill;

Wild Spirit, which art moving everywhere;
Destroyer and preserver; hear, O hear!

II

Thou on whose stream, 'mid the steep sky's
    commotion,
    Loose clouds like earth's decaying leaves are
    shed,
Shook from the tangled boughs of heaven and
    ocean,

    Angels of rain and lightning! there are spread

On the blue surface of thine airy surge,
   Like the bright hair uplifted from the head

Of some fierce Maenad, even from the dim
      verge
   Of the horizon to the zenith's height,
The locks of the approaching storm. Thou
      dirge

Of the dying year, to which this closing
      night
Will be the dome of a vast sepulchre,
   Vaulted with all thy congregated might

Of vapors, from whose solid atmosphere
Black rain, and fire, and hail will burst: O
      hear!

III
Thou who didst waken from his summer
      dreams
   The blue Mediterranean, where he lay.
Lulled by the coil of his crystalline streams,

   Beside a pumice isle in Baiae's bay,
And saw in sleep old palaces and towers
   Quivering within the wave's intenser day,

All overgrown with azure moss, and flowers
   So sweet, the sense faints picturing them!

138

Thou
For whose path the Atlantic's level powers

Cleave themselves into chasms, while far
below
The sea-blooms and the oozy woods which
wear
The sapless foliage of the ocean, know

Thy voice, and suddenly grow gray with fear,
And tremble and despoil themselves: O heart

IV
If I were a dead leaf thou mightest bear;
If I were a swift cloud to fly with thee;
A wave to pant beneath thy power, and share

The impulse of thy strength, only less free
Than thou, O uncontrollable! If even
I were as in my boyhood, and could be

The comrade of thy wanderings over heaven,
As then, when to outstrip thy skiey speed
Scarce seemed a vision — I would ne'er have
striven

As thus with thee in prayer in my sore need.
O! lift me as a wave, a leaf, a cloud!
I fall upon the thorns of life! I bleed!

A heavy weight of hours has chained and bowed
One too like thee — tameless, and swift, and
   proud.

V

Make me thy lyre, even as the forest is:
   What if my leaves are falling like its own?
The tumult of thy mighty harmonies

   Will take from both a deep, autumnal tone,
Sweet though in sadness. Be thou, Spirit
      fierce,
   My spirit! Be thou me, impetuous one!

Drive my dead thoughts over the universe,
   Like withered leaves, to quicken a new
      birth;
And, by the incantation of this verse,

   Scatter, as from an unextinguished hearth
Ashes and sparks, my words among mankind!
   Be through my lips to unawakened earth

The trumpet of a prophecy! O Wind,
If Winter comes, Can Spring be far behind?
                              Percy Bysshe Shelley

To Night

Swiftly walk o'er the western wave,
    Spirit of Night!
Out of the misty eastern cave
Where, all the long and lone daylight,
Thou wovest dreams of joy and fear,
Which make thee terrible and dear,
    Swift be thy flight!

Wrap thy form in a mantle gray,
    Star-inwrought!
Blind with thine hair the eyes of Day;
Kiss her until she be wearied out,
Then wander o'er city, and sea, and land,
Touching all with thine opiate wand —
    Come, long-sought!

When I arose and saw the dawn,
    I sighed for thee;
When light rode high, and the dew was gone,
And noon lay heavy on flower and tree,
And the weary Day turned to his rest,

Lingering like an unloved guest,
    I sighed for thee.

Thy brother Death came, and cried,
    "Would'st thou me?"
Thy sweet child Sleep, the filmy-eyed,

Murmured like a noontide bee,
  "Shall I nestle near thy side?
  Would'st thou me?" — And I replied,
  "No, not thee."

Death will come when thou art dead,
  Soon, too soon —
Sleep will come when thou art fled;
Of neither would I ask the boon
I ask of thee, beloved Night —
Swift be thine approaching flight,
  Come soon, soon!
                    Percy Bysshe Shelley

To a Skylark

Hail to thee, blithe spirit!
  Bird thou never wert,
That from heaven, or near it,
  Pourest thy full heart
In profuse strains of unpremeditated art.

Higher still and higher,
  From the earth thou springest
Like a cloud of fire;
  The blue deep thou wingest,
And singing still dost soar, and soaring ever
  singest.

In the golden lightning
   Of the sunken sun,
O'er which clouds are bright'ning,
   Thou dost float and run;
Like an unbodied joy whose race is just begun.

The pale purple even
   Melts around thy flight;
Like a star of heaven
   In the broad daylight
Thou art unseen, but yet I hear thy shrill
   delight.

Keen as are the arrows
   Of that silver sphere,
Whose intense lamp narrows
   In the white dawn clear,
Until we hardly see, we feel that it is there.

All the earth and air
   With thy voice is loud,
As, when night is bare,
   From one lonely cloud
The moon rains out her beams, and heaven is
   overflowed.

What thou art we know not;
   What is most like thee?
From rainbow clouds there flow not
   Drops so bright to see

As from thy presence showers a rain of
    melody.

    Like a poet hidden
      In the light of thought,
    Singing hymns unbidden
      Till the world is wrought
To sympathy with hopes and fears it heeded
    not:

    Like a high-born maiden
      In a palace tower,
    Soothing her love-laden
      Soul in secret hour
With music sweet as love, which overflows her
    bower:

    Like a glow-worm golden
      In a dell of dew,
    Scattering unbeholden
      Its aerial hue
Among the flowers and grass, which screen it
    from the view:

    Like a rose embowered
      In its own green leaves,
    By warm winds deflowered,
      Till the scent' it gives
Makes faint with too much sweet these heavy
    winged thieves:

Sound of vernal showers
   On the twinkling grass,
Rain-awakened flowers,
   All that ever was
Joyous, and clear, and fresh, thy music doth
      surpass.

Teach us, sprite or bird,
   What sweet thoughts are thine:
I have never heard
   Praise of love or wine
That panted forth a flood of rapture so divine.

Chorus hymeneal,
   Or triumphal chaunt,
Matched with thine would be all
   But an empty vaunt —
A thing wherein we feel there is some hidden
      want.

What objects are the fountains
   Of thy happy strain?
What fields, or waves, or mountains?
   What shapes of sky or plain?
What love of thine own kind? what ignorance
      of pain?

With thy clear keen joyance
   Languor cannot be:
Shadow of annoyance

Never came near thee:
Thou lovest; but ne'er knew love's sad satiety.

Waking or asleep,
  Thou of death must deem
Things more true and deep
  Than we mortals dream,
Or how could thy notes flow in such a crystal
    stream?

We look before and after,
  And pine for what is not:
Our sincerest laughter
  With some pain is fraught;
Our sweetest songs are those that tell of
    saddest thought.

Yet if we could scorn
  Hate, and pride, and fear;
If we were things born
  Not to shed a tear,
I know not how thy joy we ever should come
    near.

Better than all measures
  Of delightful sound,
Better than all treasures
  That in books are found,
Thy skill to poet were, thou scorner of the
    ground!

Teach me half the gladness
    That thy brain must know,
Such harmonious madness
From my lips would flow,
The world should listen then, as I am listening
    now.

Percy Bysshe Shelley

To Autumn

Season of mists and mellow fruitfulness!
Close bosom-friend of the maturing sun;
Conspiring with him how to load and bless
With fruit the vines that round the thatch-eaves
    run;
To bend with apples the mossed cottage-trees,
And fill all fruit with ripeness to the core;
To swell the gourd, and plump the hazel shells
With a sweet kernel; to set budding more,
And still more, later flowers for the bees,
Until they think warm days will never cease,
For Summer has o'erbrimmed their clammy
    cells.

Who hath not seen thee oft amid thy store?
Sometimes whoever seeks abroad my find
Thee sitting careless on a granary floor,
Thy hair soft-lifted by the winnowing wind;
Or on a half-reaped furrow sound asleep,

Drowsed with the fume of poppies, while thy
   hook
spares the next swath and all its twined
   flowers;
And sometimes like a gleaner thou dost keep
Steady thy laden head across a brook;
Or by a cider-press, with patient look,
Thou watchest the last oozings, hours by
   hours.

Where are the songs of Spring? Ay, where are
   they?
Think not of them, thou hast thy music too,
While barred clouds bloom the soft-dying day
And touch the stubble-plains with rosy hue;
Then in a wailful choir the small gnats mourn
Among the river shallows, borne aloft
Or sinking as the light wind lives or dies;
And full-grown lambs loud bleat from hilly
   bourn;
Hedge-crickets sing, and now with treble soft
The redbreast whistles from a garden-croft,
And gathering swallows twitter in the skies.

John Keats

Daybreak

A wind came up out of the sea,
And said, "O mists, make room for me!"

It hailed the ships, and cried, "Sail on,
Ye mariners, the night is gone!"

And hurried landward far away,
Crying, "Awake! it is the day!"

It said unto the forest, "Shout!
Hang all your leafy banners out!"

It touched the wood-bird's folded wing,
And said, "O bird, awake and sing!"

And o'er the farms, "O chanticleer,
Your clarion blow, the day is near!"

It whispered to the fields of corn,
"Bow down, and hail the coming morn!"

It shouted through the belfry-tower,
"Awake, O bell! proclaim the hour."

It crossed the churchyard with a sigh,
And said, "Not yet! in quiet lie."
Henry Wadsworth Longfellow

Snow-flakes

Out of the bosom of the Air,
  Out of the cloud-folds of her garments
    shaken,
Over the woodlands brown and bare,
  Over the harvest-fields forsaken,
    Silent, and soft, and slow
    Descends the snow.

Even as our cloudy fancies take
  Suddenly shape in some divine expression,
Even as the troubled heart doth make
  In the white countenance confession,
    The troubled sky reveals
    The grief it feels.

This is the poem of the air,
  Slowly in silent syllables recorded;
This is the secret of despair,
  Long in its cloudy bosom hoarded,
    Now whispered and revealed
    To wood and field.
Henry Wadsworth Longfellow

Nature

As a fond mother, when the day is o'er,
  Leads by the hand her little child to bed,
  Half willing, half reluctant to be led,
And leave his broken playthings on the floor,
Still gazing at them through the open door,
  Nor wholly reassured and comforted
  By promises of others in their stead,
Which, though more splendid, may not please
      him more;
So Nature deals with us, and takes away
  Our playthings one by one, and by the hand
    Leads us to rest so gently, that we go
Scarce knowing if we wish to go or stay,
  Being too full of sleep to understand
    How far the unknown transcends the what
    we know.
                    Henry Wadsworth Longfellow

Fragment

Flower in the crannied wall,
I pluck you out of the crannies,
I hold you here, root and all, in my hand,
Little flower — but *if* I could understand
What you are, 'root and all, and all in all,
I should know what God and man is.
                    Alfred Tennyson

When I Heard the Learn'd Astronomer

When I heard the learn'd astronomer,
When the proofs, the figures, were ranged in
   columns before me,
When I was shown the charts and diagrams, to
   add, divide, and measure them,
When I sitting heard the astronomer where he
   lectured with much applause in the lecture-
   room,
How soon unaccountable I became tired and
   sick,
Till rising and gliding out I wander'd off by
   myself,
In the mystical moist night-air, and from time
   to time,
Look'd up in perfect silence at the stars.

Walt Whitman

Home Thoughts, from Abroad

Oh, to be in England
Now that April's there,
And whoever wakes in England
Sees, some morning, unaware,
That the lowest boughs and the brushwood
   sheaf
Round the elm-tree bole are in tiny leaf,

While the chaffinch sings on the orchard bough
In England — now!

And after April, when May follows
And the white-throat builds, and all the
    swallows!
Hark, where my blossomed pear-tree in the
    hedge
Leans to the field and scatters on the clover
Blossoms and dewdrops — at the bent spray's
    edge —
That's the wise thrush: he sings each song
    twice over,

Lest you should think he never could recapture
The first fine careless rapture!
And though the fields look rough with hoary
    dew,
All will be gay when noontide wakes anew
The buttercups, the little children's dower
— Far brighter than this gaudy melon-flower!

Robert Browning

The Chambered Nautilus

This is the ship of pearl, which, poets feign,
    Sails the unshadowed main, —
    The venturous bark that flings
On the sweet summer wind its purpled wings

In gulfs enchanted, where the Siren sings,
    And coral reefs lie bare,
Where the cold sea-maids rise to sun their
      streaming hair.

Its webs of living gauze no more unfurl;
    Wrecked is the ship of pearl!
    And every chambered cell,
Where its dim dreaming life was wont to
      dwell,
As the frail tenant shaped his growing shell,
    Before thee lies revealed, —
Its irised ceiling rent, its sunless crypt
      unsealed!

Year after year beheld the silent toil
    That spread his lustrous coil;
    Still, as the spiral grew,
He left the past year's dwelling for the new,
Stole with soft step its shining archway
      through,
    Built up its idle door,
Stretched in his last-found home, and knew the
      old no more.

Thanks for the heavenly message brought by
      thee,
    Child of the wandering sea,
    Cast from her lap, forlorn!
From thy dead lips a clearer note is born

Than ever Triton blew from wreathed horn!
　While on mine ear it rings,
Through the deep caves of thought I hear a
　　voice that sings —

Build thee more stately mansions, O my soul,
　As the swift seasons roll!
　Leave thy low-vaulted past!
Let each new temple, nobler than the last,
Shut thee from heaven with a dome more vast,
　Till thou at length art free,
Leaving thine outgrown shell by life's
　　unresting sea!

Oliver Wendell Holmes

Dover Beach

The sea is calm to-night.
The tide is full, the moon lies fair
Upon the straits; — on the French coast the
　light
Gleams and is gone; the cliffs of England
　stand,
Glimmering and vast, out in the tranquil bay.
Come to the window, sweet is the night-air!
Only, from the long line of spray
Where the sea meets the moon-blanch'd sand,
Listen! you hear the grating roar

Of pebbles which the waves draw back, and
  fling,
At their return, up the high strand,
Begin, and cease, and then again begin,
With tremulous cadence slow, and bring
The eternal note of sadness in.

Sophocles long ago
Heard it on the Ægean, and it brought
Into his mind the turbid ebb and flow
Of human misery; we
Find also in the sound a thought,
Hearing it by this distant northern sea.

The sea of faith
Was once, too, at the full, and round earth's
  shore
Lay like the folds of a bright girdle furl'd
But now I only hear
Its melancholy, long, withdrawing roar,
Retreating, to the breath
Of the night-wind, down the vast edges drear
And naked shingles of the world.

Ah, love, let us be true
To one another! for the world, which seems
To lie before us like a land of dreams,
So various, so beautiful, so new,

Hath really neither joy, nor love, nor light,
Nor certitude, nor peace, nor help for pain;
And we are here as on a darkling plain
Swept with confused alarms of struggle and
    flight,
Where ignorant armies clash by night.

Matthew Arnold

The Darkling Thrush

I leaned upon a coppice gate
    When frost was specter-gray,
    And winter's dregs made desolate
    The weakening eye of day.
The tangled bine-stems scored the sky
    Like strings from broken lyres,
And all mankind that haunted nigh
    Had sought their household fires.

The land's sharp features seemed to be
    The Century's corpse outleant;
His crypt the cloudy canopy,
    The wind his death-lament.
The ancient pulse of germ and birth
    Was shrunken hard and dry,
And every spirit upon earth
    Seemed fervorless as I.

At once a voice burst forth among
   The bleak twigs overhead
In a full-hearted evensong
   Of joy unlimited;
An aged thrush, frail, gaunt and small,
   In blast-beruffled plume,
Had chosen thus to fling his soul
   Upon the growing gloom.

So little cause for carolings
   Of such ecstatic sound
Was written on terrestrial things
   Afar or nigh around,
That I could think there trembled through
   His happy good-night air
Some blessed hope, whereof he knew
   And I was unaware,

                    Thomas Hardy

A Narrow Fellow in the Grass

A narrow Fellow in the Grass
Occasionally rides —
You may have met Him — did you not
His notice sudden is —

The Grass divides as with a Comb —
A spotted shaft is seen —

And then it closes at your feet
And opens further on —

He likes a Boggy Acre
A Floor too cool for Corn —
Yet when A Boy, and Barefoot —
I more than once at Noon
Have passed, I thought, a Whip lash
Unbraiding in the Sun
When stooping to secure it
It wrinkled, and was gone —

Several of Nature's People
I know, and they know me —
I feel for them a transport
of cordiality —

But never met this Fellow
Attended, or alone
Without a tighter breathing
And Zero at the Bone —

Emily Dickinson

September

The golden-rod is yellow;
    The corn is turning brown;
The trees in apple orchards
    With fruit are bending down.

The gentian's bluest fringes
　　Are curling in the sun;
In dusty pods the milkweed
　　Its hidden silk has spun.

The sedges flaunt their harvest,
　　In every meadow nook;
And asters by the brook-side
　　Make asters in the brook,

From dewy lanes at morning
　　The grapes' sweet odors rise;
At noon the roads all flutter
　　With yellow butterflies.

By all these lovely tokens
　　September days are here,
With summer's best of weather,
　　And autumn's best of cheer.

But none of all this beauty
　　Which floods the earth and air
Is unto me the secret
　　Which makes September fair.

'Tis a thing which I remember;
　　To name it thrills me yet:
One day of one September
　　I never can forget.

Helen Hunt Jackson

When the Frost Is on the Punkin

When the frost is on the punkin and the
    fodder's in the shock,
And you hear the kyouck and gobble of the
    struttin' turkeycock,
And the clackin' of the guineys, and the
    cluckin' of the hens,
And the rooster's hallylooyer as he tiptoes on
    the fence;
O, it's then's the times a feller is a-feelin' at
    his best,
With the risin' sun to greet him from a night of
    peaceful rest,
As he leaves the house, bareheaded, and goes
    out to feed the stock,
When the frost is on the punkin and the
    fodder's in the shock.

They's something kindo' harty-like about the
    atmusfere
When the heat of summer's over and the
    coolin' fall is here —
Of course we miss the flowers, and the
    blossoms on the trees,
And the mumble of the hummin'-birds and
    buzzin' of the bees;
But the air's so appetizin'; and the landscape
    through the haze

Of a crisp and sunny morning of the airly
    autumn days
Is a pictur' that no painter has the colorin' to
    mock —
When the frost is on the punkin and the
    fodder's in the shock.

The husky, rusty russel of the tossels of the
    corn,
And the raspin' of the tangled leaves, as
    golden as the morn;
The stubble in the furries — kindo' lonesome-
    like, but still
A-preachin' sermuns to us of the barns they
    growed to fill;
The strawstack in the medder, and the reaper
    in the shed;
The hosses in theyr stalls below — the clover
    overhead! —
O, it sets my hart a-clickin' like the tickin' of
    a clock,
When the frost in on the punkin and the
    fodder's in the shock.

Then your apples all is getherd, and the ones a
    feller keeps
Is poured around the celler-floor in red and
    yeller heaps;
And your cider-makin's over, and your
    wimmern-folks is through

With their mince and apple-butter, and theyr
    souse and saussage, too! . . .
I don't know how to tell it — but ef sich a
    thing could be
As the Angels wantin' boardin', and they'd
    call around on *me* —
I'd want to 'commodate 'em — all the whole-
    indurin' flock —
When the frost is on the punkin and the
    fodder's in the shock.

James Whitcomb Riley

The Lake Isle of Innisfree

I will arise and go now, and go to Innisfree,
And a small cabin build there, of clay and
    wattles made;
Nine bean rows will I have there, a hive for
    the honey bee,
    And live alone in the bee-loud glade.

And I shall have some peace there, for peace
    comes dropping slow,
Dropping from the veils of the morning to
    where the cricket sings;
There midnight's all a glimmer, and noon a
    purple glow,
    And evening full of the linnet's wings.

I will arise and go now, for always night and
    day
I hear lake water lapping with low sounds by
    the shore;
While I stand on the roadway, or on the
    pavements gray,
    I hear it in the deep heart's core.
                        William Butler Yeats

Day That I Have Loved

Tenderly, day that I have loved, I close your
        eyes,
    And smooth your quiet brow, and fold your
        thin dead hands.
The grey veils of the half-light deepen; colour
        dies
    I bear you, a light burden, to the shrouded
        sands,

Where lies your waiting boat, by wreaths of
        the sea's making
    Mist-garlanded, with all grey weeds of the
        water crowned.
There you'll be laid, past fear of sleep or hope
        of waking;
    And over the unmoving sea, without a
        sound,

Faint hands will row you outward, out beyond
      our sight,
   Us with stretched arms and empty eyes on
      the far-gleaming
And marble sand . . .
      Beyond the shifting cold twilight,
   Further than laughter goes, or tears, further
      than dreaming.

There'll be no port, no dawn-lit islands! But
      the drear
   Waste darkening, and, at length, flame
      ultimate on the deep.
Oh, the last fire — and you, unkissed,
      unfriended there!
   Oh, the lone way's red ending, and we not
      there to weep!

(We found you pale and quiet, and strangely
      crowned with flowers,
   Lovely and secret as a child. You came with
      us,
Came happily, hand in hand with the young
      dancing hours,
   High on the downs at dawn!) Void now and
      tenebrous,

The grey sands curve before me . . .
      From the inland meadows,

Fragrant of June and clover, floats the dark,
    and fills
The hollow sea's dead face with little creeping
    shadows,
    And the white silence brims the hollow of
    the hills.

Close in the nest is folded every weary wing,
    Hushed all the joyful voices; and we, who
    held you dear,
Eastward we turn, and homeward, alone,
    remembering . . .
    Day that I loved, day that I loved, the Night
    is here!

Rupert Brooke

Sea Fever

I must go down to the seas again, to the lonely
    sea and the sky,
And all I ask is a tall ship and a star to steer
    her by;
And the wheel's kick and the wind's song and
    the white sail's shaking,
And a gray mist on the sea's face, and a gray
    dawn breaking.

I must go down to the seas again, for the call
    of the running tide

Is a wild call and a clear call that may not be
    denied;
And all I ask is a windy day with the white
    clouds flying,
And the flung spray and the blown spume, and
    the sea-gulls crying.

I must go down to the seas again, to the
    vagrant gipsy life,
To the gull's way and the whale's way where
    the wind's like a whetted knife;
And all I ask is a merry yarn from a laughing
    fellow-rover,
And quiet sleep and a sweet dream when the
    long trick's over.

John Masefield

The West Wind

It's a warm wind, the west wind, full of birds'
    cries;
I never hear the west wind but tears are in my
    eyes.
For it comes from the west lands, the old
    brown hills,
And April's in the west wind, and daffodils.

It's a fine land, the west land, for hearts as
    tired as mine,

Apple orchards blossom there, and the air's
  like wine.
There is cool green grass there, where men
  may lie at rest;
And the thrushes are in song there, fluting
  from the nest.

"Will you not come home, brother? You have
  been long away.
It's April, and blossom time, and white is the
  spray:
And bright is the sun, brother, and warm is the
  rain;
Will you not come home, brother, home to us
  again?

"The young corn is green, brother, where the
  rabbits run;
It's blue sky, and white clouds, and warm rain
  and sun.
It's song to a man's soul, brother, fire to a
  man's brain,
To hear the wild bees and see the merry spring
  again.

"Larks are singing in the west, brother, above
  the green wheat,
So will you not come home, brother, and rest
  your tired feet?
I've a balm for bruised hearts, brother, sleep

for aching eyes,"
Says the warm wind, the west wind, full of
 birds' cries.

It's the white road westwards is the road I
 must tread
To the green grass, the cool grass, and rest for
 heart and head,
To the violets and the brown brooks and the
 thrushes' song
In the fine land, the west land, the land where
 I belong.

John Masefield

Reveille

Wake! the silver dusk returning
 Up the beach of darkness brims,
And the ship of sunrise burning
 Strands upon the eastern rims.

Wake! the vaulted shadow shatters,
 Trampled to the door it spanned,
And the tent of night in tatters
 Straws the sky-pavilioned land.

Up, lad, up! 'Tis late for lying.
 Hear the drums of morning play;

Hark, the empty highways crying,
  "Who'll beyond the hills away?"

Towns and countries woo together,
  Forelands beacon, belfries call;
Never lad that trod on leather
  Lived to feast his heart with all.

Up, lad! Thews that lie and cumber
  Sunlit pallets never thrive;
Morns abed and daylight slumber
  Were not meant for man alive.

Clay lies still, but blood's a rover;
  Breath's a ware that will not keep.
Up, lad! When the journey's over
  There'll be time enough to sleep.
                    (From *A Shropshire Lad*)
                    A. E. Housman

Puritan Sonnet

Down to the Puritan marrow of my bones
There's something in this richness that I hate.
I love the look, austere, immaculate,
Of landscapes drawn in pearly monotones.
There's something in my very blood that owns
Bare hills, cold silver on a sky of slate,
A thread of water, churned to milky spate

Streaming through slanted pastures fenced with
  stones.

I love those skies, thin blue or snowy gray,
Those fields sparse-planted, rendering meager
  sheaves;
That spring, briefer than apple-blossom's
  breath,
Summer, so much too beautiful to stay,
Swift autumn, like a bonfire of leaves,
And sleepy winter, like the sleep of death.

                         Elinor Wylie

Velvet Shoes

Let us walk in the white snow
  In a soundless space;
With footsteps quiet and slow,
  At a tranquil pace,
  Under veils of white lace.

I shall go shod in silk,
  And you in wool,
White as a white cow's milk,
  More beautiful
  Than the breast of a gull.

We shall walk through the still town
  In a windless peace;

We shall step upon white down,
  Upon silver fleece,
  Upon softer than these.

We shall walk in velvet shoes:
  Wherever we go
Silence will fall like dews
  On white silence below.
  We shall walk in the snow.
                              Elinor Wylie

Trees

(For Mrs. Henry Mills Alden)

I think that I shall never see
A poem lovely as a tree.

A tree whose hungry mouth is prest
Against the earth's sweet flowing breast;

A tree that looks at God all day,
And lifts her leafy arms to pray;

A tree that may in Summer wear
A nest of robins in her hair;

Upon whose bosom snow has lain;
Who intimately lives with rain.

Poems are made by fools like me,
But only God can make a tree.
Joyce Kilmer

Fog

The fog comes
on little cat feet.

It sits looking
over harbor and city
on silent haunches
and then moves on.
Carl Sandburg

Acquainted with the Night

I have been one acquainted with the night,
I have walked out in rain — and back in rain.
I have outwalked the furthest city light.

I have looked down the saddest city lane.
I have passed by the watchman on the beat
And dropped my eyes, unwilling to explain.

I have stood still and stopped the sound of feet
When far away an interrupted cry
Came over houses from another street.

But not to call me back or say good-bye;
And further still at an unearthly height,
One luminary clock against the sky

Proclaimed the time was neither wrong nor
   right
I have been one acquainted with the night.

Robert Frost

After Apple Picking

My long two-pointed ladder's sticking through
   a tree
Toward heaven still,
And there's a barrel that I didn't fill
Beside it, and there may be two or three
Apples I didn't pick upon some bough.
But I am done with apple picking now.
Essence of winter sleep is on the night,
The scent of apples: I am drowsing off.
I cannot rub the strangeness from my sight
I got from looking through a pane of glass
I skimmed this morning from the drinking
   trough
And held against the world of hoary grass.
It melted, and I let it fall and break.
But I was well
Upon my way to sleep before it fell,
And I could tell

What form my dreaming was about to take.
Magnified apples appear and disappear
Stem end and blossom end,
And every fleck of russet showing clear.
My instep arch not only keeps the ache,
It keeps the pressure of a ladder round.
I feel the ladder sway as the boughs bend.
And I keep hearing from the cellar bin
The rumbling sound
Of load on load of apples coming in.
For I have had too much
Of apple picking: I am overtired
Of the great harvest I myself desired.
There were ten thousand thousand fruit to
   touch,
Cherish in hand, lift down, and not let fall.
For all
That struck the earth,
No matter if not bruised or spiked with
   stubble,
Went surely to the cider-apple heap
As of no worth.
One can see what will trouble
This sleep of mine, whatever sleep it is.
Were he not gone,
The woodchuck could say whether it's like his
Long sleep, as I describe its coming on,
Or just some human sleep.

Robert Frost

Birches

When I see birches bend to left and right
Across the lines of straighter darker trees,
I like to think some boy's been swinging them.
But swinging doesn't bend them down to stay.
Ice-storms do that. Often you must have seen
   them
Loaded with ice a sunny winter morning
After a rain. They click upon themselves
As the breeze rises, and turn many-colored
As the stir cracks and crazes their enamel.
Soon the sun's warmth makes them shed
   crystal shells
Shattering and avalanching on the
   snow-crust —
Such heaps of broken glass to sweep away
You'd think the inner dome of heaven had
   fallen.
They are dragged to the withered bracken by
   the load,
And they seem not to break; though once they
   are bowed
So low for long, they never right themselves:
You may see their trunks arching in the woods
Years afterwards, trailing their leaves on the
   ground
Like girls on hands and knees that throw their
   hair
Before them over their heads to dry in the sun.

But I was going to say when Truth broke in
With all her matter-of-fact about the ice-storm
I should prefer to have some boy bend them
As he went out and in to fetch the cows —
Some boy too far from town to learn baseball,
Whose only play was what he found himself,
Summer or winter, and could play alone.
One by one he subdued his father's trees
By riding them down over and over again
Until he took the stiffness out of them,
And not one but hung limp, not one was left
For him to conquer. He learned all there was
To learn about not launching out too soon
And so not carrying the tree away
Clear to the ground. He always kept his poise
To the top branches, climbing carefully
With the same pains you use to fill a cup
Up to the brim, and even above the brim.
Then he flung outward, feet first, with a swish,
Kicking his way down through the air to the
    ground.
So was I once myself a swinger of birches.
And so I dream of going back to be.
It's when I'm weary of considerations,
And life is too much like a pathless wood
Where your face burns and tickles with the
    cobwebs
Broken across it, and eye is weeping
From a twig's having lashed across it open:
I'd like to get away from earth awhile

And then come back to it and begin over.
May no fate willfully misunderstand me
And half grant what I wish and snatch me
    away
Not to return. Earth's the right place for love:
I don't know where it's likely to go better.
I'd like to go by climbing a birch tree,
And climb black branches up a snow-white
    trunk
Toward heaven, till the tree could bear no
    more,
But dipped its top and set me down again.
That would be good both going and coming
    back.
One could do worse than be a swinger of
    birches.

                          Robert Frost

Stopping by Woods on a Snowy Evening

Whose woods these are I think I know.
His house is in the village though;
He will not see me stopping here
To watch his woods fill up with snow.

My little horse must think it queer
To stop without a farmhouse near

Between the woods and frozen lake
The darkest evening of the year.

He gives his harness bells a shake
To ask if there is some mistake.
The only other sound's the sweep
Of easy wind and downy flake.

The woods are lovely, dark and deep,
But I have promises to keep,
And miles to go before I sleep,
And miles to go before I sleep.

Robert Frost

Snow

The room was suddenly rich and the great bay-
    window was
Spawning snow and pink roses against it
Soundlessly collateral and incompatible:
World is suddener than we fancy it.

World is crazier and more of it than we think,
Incorrigibly plural. I peel and portion
A tangerine and spit the pips and feel
The drunkenness of things being various.

And the fire flames with a bubbling sound for
    world

Is more spiteful and gay than one supposes —
On the tongue on the eyes on the ears in the
   palms of your hands —
There is more than glass between the snow and
   the huge roses.

Louis MacNeice

Fern Hill

Now as I was young and easy under the apple
      boughs
About the lilting house and happy as the grass
      was green,
   The night above the dingle starry,
      Time let me hail and climb
      Golden in the heydays of his eyes,
And honored among wagons I was prince of
      the apple towns
And once below a time I lordly had the trees
      and leaves
      Trail with daisies and barley
      Down the rivers of the windfall light.

And as I was green and carefree, famous
      among the barns
About the happy yard and singing as the farm
      was home,
   In the sun that is young once only,

180

Time let me play and be
Golden in the mercy of his means,
And green and golden I was huntsman and
herdsman, the calves
Sang to my horn, the foxes on the hills barked
clear and cold,
And the sabbath rang slowly
In the pebbles of the holy streams.

All the sun long it was running, it was lovely,
the hay-
Fields high as the house, the tunes from the
chimneys, it was air
And playing, lovely and watery
And fire green as grass.
And nightly under the simple stars
As I rode to sleep the owls were bearing the
farm away,
All the moon long I heard, blessed among
stables, the nightjars
Flying with the ricks, and horses
Flashing into the dark

And then to awake, and the farm, like a
wanderer white
With the dew, come back, the cock on his
shoulder: it was all
Shining, it was Adam and maiden,
The sky gathered again
And the sun grew round that very day.

So it must have been after the birth of the
      simple light
In the first, spinning place, the spellbound
      horses walking warm
    Out of the whinnying green stable
      On to the fields of praise.

And honored among foxes and pheasants by
      the gay house
Under the new-made clouds and happy as the
      heart was long
    In the sun born over and over,
      I ran my heedless ways,
    My wishes raced through the house-high hay
And nothing I cared, at my sky blue trades,
      that time allows
In all his tuneful turning so few and such
      morning songs
    Before the children green and golden
      Follow him out of grace.

Nothing I cared, in the lamb white days, that
      time would take me
Up to the swallow-thronged loft by the shadow
      of my hand,
    In the moon that is always rising,
      Nor that riding to sleep
    I should hear him fly with the high fields
And wake to the farm forever fled from the
      childless land.

Oh as I was young and easy in the mercy of
    his means,
Time held me green and dying
Though I sang in my chains like the sea.
Dylan Thomas

Childhood and Youth

Sonnet LX

Like as the waves make towards the pebbled
    shore,
So do our minutes hasten to their end;
Each changing place with that which goes
    before,
In sequent toil all forwards do contend.
Nativity, once in the main of light,
Crawls to maturity, wherewith being crowned,
Crookèd eclipses 'gainst his glory fight,
And Time that gave doth now his gift
    confound.
Time doth transfix the flourish set on youth
And delves the parallels in beauty's brow,
Feeds on the rarities of nature's truth,
And nothing stands but for his scythe to mow:
  And yet to times in hope my verse shall
    stand,
  Praising thy worth, despite his cruel hand.
William Shakespeare

Cradle Song

Sleep, sleep, beauty bright,
Dreaming in the joys of night;
Sleep, sleep; in thy sleep
Little sorrows sit and weep.

Sweet babe, in thy face
Soft desires I can trace,
Secret joys and secret smiles,
Little pretty infant wiles.

As thy softest limbs I feel
Smiles as of the morning steal
O'er thy cheek, and o'er thy breast
Where thy little heart doth rest.

O the cunning wiles that creep
In thy little heart asleep!
When thy little heart doth wake,
Then the dreadful night shall break.
William Blake

The Old Oaken Bucket

How dear to my heart are the scenes of my
    childhood,
    When fond recollection presents them to
    view!

The orchard, the meadow, the deep tangled
  wildwood,
    And every loved spot which my infancy
    knew,
The wide-spreading pond and the mill that
  stood by it,
    The bridge and the rock where the cataract
    fell;
The cot of my father, the dairy house nigh it,
  And e'en the rude bucket that hung in the
  well.

That moss-covered bucket I hailed as a
  treasure,
    For often at noon, when returned from the
    field,
I found it the source of an exquisite pleasure,
  The purest and sweetest that nature can
  yield.
How ardent I seized it, with hands that were
  glowing,
    And quick to the white-pebbled bottom it
    fell.
Then soon, with the emblem of truth
  overflowing,
    And dripping with coolness, it rose from the
    well.

How sweet from the green, mossy brim to
    receive it,
    As, poised on the curb, it inclined to my
      lips!
Not a full, blushing goblet could tempt me to
    leave it,
    Tho' filled with the nectar that Jupiter sips.
And now, far removed from the loved
    habitation,
    The tear of regret will intrusively swell,
As fancy reverts to my father's plantation,
    And sighs for the bucket that hung in the
      well.

Samuel Woodworth

A Visit from St. Nicholas

'Twas the night before Christmas, when all
    through the house
Not a creature was stirring, not even a mouse;
The stockings were hung by the chimney with
    care,
In hopes that St. Nicholas soon would be there;
The children were nestled all snug in their
    beds,
While visions of sugar-plums danced in their
    heads;
And mamma in her kerchief, and I in my cap,

Had just settled our brains for a long winter's
    nap, —
When out on the lawn there arose such a
    clatter,
I sprang from my bed to see what was the
    matter.
Away to the window I flew like a flash,
Tore open the shutters and threw up the sash.
The moon on the breast of the new-fallen snow
Gave a lustre of midday to objects below;
When what to my wondering eyes should
    appear,
But a miniature sleigh and eight tiny reindeer,
With a little old driver, so lively and quick
I knew in a moment it must be St. Nick.
More rapid than eagles his coursers they
    came,
And he whistled and shouted, and called them
    by name:
"Now, Dasher! now, Dancer! Now, Prancer
    and Vixen!
On, Comet! on, Cupid! on, Donder and
    Blitzen!
To the top of the porch, to the top of the wall!
Now dash away, dash away, dash away all!"
As dry leaves that before the wild hurricane
    fly,
When they meet with an obstacle, mount to the
    sky,
So up to the house-top the coursers they flew,

With the sleigh full of toys, — and St.
  Nicholas too.
And then in a twinkling I heard on the roof
The prancing and pawing of each little
  hoof.
As I drew in my head, and was turning
  around,
Down the chimney St. Nicholas came with a
  bound.
He was dressed all in fur from his head to his
  foot,
And his clothes were all tarnished with ashes
  and soot;
A bundle of toys he had flung on his back,
And he looked like a pedlar just opening his
  pack.
His eyes, how they twinkled! his dimples, how
  merry!
His cheeks were like roses, his nose like a
  cherry;
His droll little mouth was drawn up like a
  bow,
And the beard on his chin was as white as the
  snow.
The stump of a pipe he held tight in his teeth,
And the smoke it encircled his head like a
  wreath.
He had a broad face and a little round belly
That shook, when he laughed, like a bowl full
  of jelly.

He was chubby and plump, — a right jolly old
  elf;
And I laughed, when I saw him, in spite of
  myself.
A wink of his eye and a twist of his head
Soon gave me to know I had nothing to dread.
He spoke not a word, but went straight to his
  work,
And filled all the stockings; then turned with a
  jerk,
And laying his finger aside of his nose,
And giving a nod, up the chimney he rose.
He sprang to his sleigh, to his team gave a
  whistle,
And away they all flew like the down of a
  thistle;
But I heard him exclaim, ere he drove out of
  sight,
"Happy Christmas to all, and to all a good-
  night!"

Clement Clarke Moore

I Remember, I Remember

I remember, I remember,
  The house where I was born,
The little window where the sun
  Came peeping in at morn:
He never came a wink too soon,

Nor brought too long a day;
But now, I often wish the night
  Had borne my breath away.

I remember, I remember,
  The roses, red and white;
The violets and the lily-cups,
  Those flowers made of light!
The lilacs where the robin built,
  And where my brother set
The laburnum on his birthday, —
  The tree is living yet!

I remember, I remember,
  Where I was used to swing;
And thought the air must rush as fresh
  To swallows on the wing:
My spirit flew in feathers then,
  That is so heavy now,
And summer pools could hardly cool
  The fever on my brow!

I remember, I remember,
  The fir trees dark and high;
I used to think their slender tops
  Were close against the sky:
It was a childish ignorance,
  But now 'tis little joy
To know I'm farther off from heaven
  Than when I was a boy.

Thomas Hood

194

Woodman, Spare That Tree

Woodman, spare that tree!
  Touch not a single bough!
In youth it sheltered me,
  And I'll protect it now.
'Twas my forefather's hand
  That placed it near his cot;
There, woodman, let it stand,
  Thy axe shall harm it not!

That old familiar tree,
  Whose glory and renown
Are spread o'er land and sea,
  And wouldst thou hew it down?
Woodman, forbear thy stroke!
  Cut not its earth-bound ties;
O, spare that aged oak,
  Now towering to the skies!

When but an idle boy
  I sought its grateful shade;
In all their gushing joy
  Here too my sisters played.
My mother kissed me here;
  My father pressed my hand —
Forgive this foolish tear,
  But let that old oak stand!

My heart-strings round thee cling,

Close as thy bark, old friend!
Here shall the wild-bird sing,
  And still thy branches bend.
Old tree! The storm still brave!
  And, woodman, leave the spot;
While I've a hand to save,
  Thy axe shall hurt it not.
                George Pope Morris

The Children's Hour

Between the dark and the daylight,
  When the night is beginning to lower,
Comes a pause in the day's occupations,
  That is known as the Children's Hour.

I hear in the chamber above me
  The patter of little feet,
The sound of a door that is opened,
  And voices soft and sweet.

From my study I see in the lamplight,
  Descending the broad hall stair,
Grave Alice, and laughing Allegra,
  And Edith with golden hair.

A whisper, and then a silence:
  Yet I know by their merry eyes

They are plotting and planning together
   To take me by surprise.

A sudden rush from the stairway,
   A sudden raid from the hall!
By three doors left unguarded
   They enter my castle wall!

They climb up into my turret
   O'er the arms and back of my chair;
If I try to escape, they surround me;
   They seem to be everywhere.

They almost devour me with kisses,
   Their arms about me entwine,
Till I think of the Bishop of Bingen
   In his Mouse-Tower on the Rhine!

Do you think, O blue-eyed banditti,
   Because you have scaled the wall,
Such an old mustache as I am
   Is not a match for you all!

I have you fast in my fortress,
   And will not let you depart,
But put you down into the dungeon
   In the round-tower of my heart.

And there will I keep you forever,
   Yes, forever and a day,

Till the walls shall crumble to ruin
And moulder in dust away.
Henry Wadsworth Longfellow

My Lost Youth

Often I think of the beautiful town
  That is seated by the sea;
Often in thought go up and down
The pleasant streets of that dear old town,
  And my youth comes back to me.
    And a verse of a Lapland song
    Is haunting my memory still:
    "A boy's will is the wind's will,
And the thoughts of youth are long, long
      thoughts."

I can see the shadowy lines of its trees,
  And catch, in sudden gleams,
The sheen of the far-surrounding seas,
And islands that were the Hesperides
  Of all my boyish dreams.
    And the burden of that old song,
    It murmurs and whispers still:
    "A boy's will is the wind's will,
And the thoughts of youth are long, long
      thoughts."

I remember the black wharves and the slips,
  And the sea-tides tossing free;
And Spanish sailors with bearded lips,
And the beauty and mystery of the ships,
  And the magic of the sea.
    And the voice of that wayward song
    Is singing and saying still:
    "A boy's will is the wind's will,
And the thoughts of youth are long, long
    thoughts."

I remember the bulwarks by the shore,
  And the fort upon the hill;
The sunrise gun, with its hollow roar,
The drum-beat repeated o'er and o'er,
  And the bugle wild and shrill.
    And the music of that old song
    Throbs in my memory still:
    "A boy's will is the wind's will,
And the thoughts of youth are long, long
    thoughts."

I remember the sea-fight far away,
  How it thundered o'er the tide!
And the dead captains, as they lay
In their graves, o'erlooking the tranquil bay
  Where they in battle died.
    And the sound of that mournful song
    Goes through me with a thrill:
    "A boy's will is the wind's will,

And the thoughts of youth are long, long
      thoughts.''

I can see the breezy dome of groves,
  The shadows of Deering's Woods;
And the friendships old and the early loves
Come back with a Sabbath sound, as of doves
  In quiet neighborhoods.
    And the verse of that sweet old song,
    It flutters and murmurs still:
    ''A boy's will is the wind's will,
And the thoughts of youth are long, long
      thoughts.''

I remember the gleams and glooms that dart
  Across the school-boy's brain;
The song and the silence in the heart,
That in part are prophecies, and in part
  Are longings wild and vain.
    And the voice of that fitful song
    Sings on, and is never still:
    ''A boy's will is the wind's will,
And the thoughts of youth are long, long
      thoughts.''

There are things of which I may not speak;
  There are dreams that cannot die;
There are thoughts that make the strong heart
      weak,
And bring a pallor into the cheek,

And a mist before the eye.
　　And the words of that fatal song
　　Come over me like a chill:
　"A boy's will is the wind's will,
And the thoughts of youth are long, long
　　　thoughts."

Strange to me are the forms I meet
　When I visit the dear old town;
But the native air is pure and sweet,
And the trees that o'ershadow each well-known
　　　street,
　As they balance up and down,
　　Are singing the beautiful song,
　　Are sighing and whispering still:
　　"A boy's will is the wind's will,
And the thoughts of youth are long, long
　　　thoughts."

And Deering's Woods are fresh and fair,
　And with joy that is almost pain
My heart goes back to wander there,
And among the dreams of the days that were
　I find my lost youth again.
　　And the strange and beautiful song,
　　The groves are repeating it still:
　　"A boy's will is the wind's will,
And the thoughts of youth are long, long
　　　thoughts."

Henry Wadsworth Longfellow

201

The Barefoot Boy

Blessings on thee, little man,
Barefoot boy, with cheek of tan!
With thy turned-up pantaloons,
And thy merry whistled tunes;
With thy red lip, redder still
Kissed by strawberries on the hill;
With the sunshine on thy face,
Through thy torn brim's jaunty grace;
From my heart I give thee joy, —
I was once a barefoot boy!
Prince thou art, — the grown-up man
Only is republican.
Barefoot, trudging at his side,
Thou hast more than he can buy
In the reach of ear and eye, —
Outward sunshine, inward joy:
Blessings on thee, barefoot boy!

Oh for boyhood's painless play,
Sleep that wakes in laughing day,
Health that mocks the doctor's rules,
Knowledge never learned of schools,
Of the wild bee's morning chase,
Of the wild flower's time and place,
Flight of fowl and habitude
Of the tenants of the wood;
How the tortoise bears his shell,
How the woodchuck digs his cell,

And the ground-mole sinks his well;
How the robin feeds her young,
How the oriole's nest is hung;
Where the whitest lilies blow,
Where the freshest berries grow,
Where the ground-nut trails its vine,
Where the wood-grape's chusters shine;
Of the black wasp's cunning way,
Mason of his walls of clay,
And the architectural plans
Of gray hornet artisans!
For, eschewing books and tasks,
Nature answers all he asks;
Hand in hand with her he walks,
Face to face with her he talks,
Part and parcel of her joy, —
Blessings on the barefoot boy!

Oh for boyhood's time of June,
Crowding years in one brief moon,
When all things I heard or saw,
Me, their master, waited for.
I was rich in flowers and trees,
Humming-birds and honey-bees;
For my sport the squirrel played,
Plied the snouted mole his spade;
For my taste the blackberry cone
Purpled over hedge and stone;
Laughed the brook for my delight
Through the day and through the night,

Whispering at the garden wall,
Talked with me from fall to fall;
Mine the sand-rimmed pickerel pond
Mine the walnut slopes beyond,
Mine, on bending orchard trees,
Apples of Hesperides!
Still as my horizon grew,
Larger grew my riches too;
All the world I saw or knew
Seemed a complex Chinese toy,
Fashioned for a barefoot boy!

Oh for festal dainties spread,
Like my bowl of milk and bread;
Pewter spoon and bowl of wood,
On the door-stone, gray and rude!
O'er me, like a regal tent,
Cloudy-ribbed, the sunset bent,
Purple-curtained, fringed with gold,
Looped in many a wind-swung fold;
While for music came the play
Of the pied frogs' orchestra;
And, to light the noisy choir,
Lit the fly his lamp of fire.
I was monarch: pomp and joy
Waited on the barefoot boy!

Cheerily, then, my little man,
Live and laugh, as boyhood can!
Though the flinty slopes be hard,

Stubble-speared the new-mown sward,
Every morn shall lead thee through
Fresh baptisms of the dew;
Every evening from thy feet
Shall the cool wind kiss the heat:
All too soon these feet must hide
In the prison cells of pride,
Lose the freedom of the sod,
Like a colt's for work be shod,
Made to tread the mills of toil,
Up and down in ceaseless moil:
Happy if their track be found
Never on forbidden ground;
Happy if they sink not in
Quick and treacherous sands of sin.
Ah! that thou couldst know thy joy,
Ere it passes, barefoot boy!

John Greenleaf Whittier

In School-Days

Still sits the school-house by the road,
  A ragged beggar sunning;
Around it still the sumachs grow,
  And blackberry-vines are running.

Within, the master's desk is seen,
  Deep scarred by raps official;

The warping floor, the battered seats,
   The jack-knife's carved initial;

The charcoal frescoes on its wall;
   Its door's worn sill, betraying
The feet that, creeping slow to school,
   Went storming out to playing!

Long years ago a winter sun
   Shone over it at setting;
Lit up its western window-panes,
   And low eaves' icy fretting.

It touched the tangled golden curls,
   And brown eyes full of grieving,
Of one who still her steps delay
   When all the school were leaving.

For near her stood the little boy
   Her childish favor singled;
His cap pulled low upon a face
   Where pride and shame were mingled.

Pushing with restless feet the snow
   To right and left, he lingered; —
As restlessly her tiny hands
   The blue-checked apron fingered.

He saw her lift her eyes; he felt
   The soft hand's light caressing,

And heard the tremble of her voice,
    As if a fault confessing.

"I'm sorry that I spelt the word:
    I hate to go above you,
Because," — the brown eyes lower fell. —
    "Because, you see, I love you!"

Still memory to a gray-haired man
    That sweet child-face is showing.
Dear girl! the grasses on her grave
    Have forty years been growing!

He lives to learn, in life's hard school,
    How few who pass above him
Lament their triumph and his loss,
    Like her, — because they love him.

John Greenleaf Whittier

Little Boy Blue

The little toy dog is covered with dust,
    But sturdy and stanch he stands;
And the little toy soldier is red with rust,
    And his musket moulds in his hands.
Time was when the little toy dog was new,
    And the soldier was passing fair;
And that was the time when our Little

Boy Blue
Kissed them and put them there.

"Now, don't you go till I come," he said,
   "And don't you make any noise!"
So, toddling off to his trundle-bed,
   He dreamt of the pretty toys;
And, as he was dreaming, an angel song
   Awakened our Little Boy Blue —
Oh! the years are many, the years are long,
   But the little toy friends are true!

Ay, faithful to Little Boy Blue they stand,
   Each in the same old place,
Awaiting the touch of a little hand,
   The smile of a little face;
And they wonder, as waiting the long years
      through
   In the dust of that little chair,
What has become of our Little Boy Blue,
   Since he kissed them and put them there.
                              Eugene Field

A Dutch Lullaby

Wynken, Blynken, and Nod one night
   Sailed off in a wooden shoe —
Sailed on a river of misty light
   Into a sea of dew.

"Where are you going, and what do you
     wish?"
  The old moon asked the three.
"We have come to fish for the herring-fish
  That live in this beautiful sea;
  Nets of silver and gold have we,"
          Said Wynken,
          Blynken,
          And Nod.

The old moon laughed and sung a song
  As they rocked in the wooden shoe,
And the wind that sped them all night long
  Ruffled the waves of dew;
The little stars were the herring-fish
  That lived in the beautiful sea;
"Now cast your nets wherever you wish,
  But never afeard are we" —
  So cried the stars to the fishermen three,
          Wynken,
          Blynken,
          And Nod.

All night long their nets they threw
  For the fish in the twinkling foam,
Then down from the sky came the wooden
     shoe,
  Bringing the fishermen home.
'T was all so pretty a sail, it seemed
  As if it could not be;

And some folks thought 't was a dream they'd
    dreamed
    Of sailing that beautiful sea.
    But I shall name you the fishermen three:
        Wynken,
        Blynken,
        And Nod.

Wynken and Blynken are two little eyes,
    And Nod is a little head,
And the wooden shoe that sailed the skies
    Is a wee one's trundle-bed;
So shut your eyes while mother sings
    Of the wonderful sights that be,
And you shall see the beautiful things
    As you rock in the misty sea
    Where the old shoe rocked the fishermen
        three —
        Wynken,
        Blynken,
        And Nod.

Eugene Field

Grief and
Death

Death, Be Not Proud

Death, be not proud, though some have called
thee
Mighty and dreadful, for thou are not so;
For those whom thou think'st thou dost
overflow
Die not, poor Death; nor yet canst thou kill
me.
From rest and sleep, which but thy picture be,
Much pleasure; then from thee much more
must flow;
And soonest our best men with thee do go —
Rest of their bones and souls' delivery!
Thou'rt slave to fate, chance, kings, and
desperate men,
And dost with poison, war, and sickness dwell;
And poppy or charms can make us sleep as
well
And better than thy stroke. Why swell'st thou
then?
One short sleep past, we wake eternally,
And Death shall be no more: Death, thou shalt
die.

John Donne

Elegy Written in a Country Churchyard

The curfew tolls the knell of parting day,
  The lowing herd winds slowly o'er the lea,
The plowman homeward plods his weary way,
  And leaves the world to darkness and to me.

Now fades the glimmering landscape on the
    sight,
  And all the air a solemn stillness holds,
Save where the beetle wheels his droning
    flight,
  And drowsy tinklings lull the distant folds:

Save that from yonder ivy-mantled tower
  The moping owl does to the moon complain
Of such as, wandering near her secret bower,
  Molest her ancient solitary reign.

Beneath those rugged elms, that yew-tree's
    shade,
  Where heaves the turf in many a moldering
    heap,
Each in his narrow cell for ever laid,
  The rude forefathers of the hamlet sleep.

The breezy call of incense-breathing morn,
  The swallow twittering from the straw-built
    shed,
The cock's shrill clarion, or the echoing horn,

No more shall rouse them from their lowly
    bed.

For them no more the blazing hearth shall
    burn,
  Or busy housewife ply her evening care:
No children run to lisp their sire's return,
  Or climb his knees the envied kiss to share.

Oft did the harvest to their sickle yield,
  Their furrow oft the stubborn glebe has
    broke:
How jocund did they drive their team afield!
  How bowed the woods beneath their sturdy
    stroke!

Let not Ambition mock their useful toil,
  Their homely joys, and destiny obscure;
Nor Grandeur hear with a disdainful smile
  The short and simple annals of the poor.

The boast of heraldry, the pomp of power,
  And all that beauty, all that wealth e'er
    gave,
Awaits alike the inevitable hour:
  The paths of glory lead but to the grave.

Nor you, ye proud, impute to these the fault
  If Memory o'er their tomb no trophies raise,
Where through the long-drawn aisle and

fretted vault
The pealing anthem swells the note of
     praise.

Can storied urn or animated bust
     Back to its mansion call the fleeting breath?
Can Honor's voice provoke the silent dust,
     Or Flattery soothe the dull cold ear of death?

Perhaps in this neglected spot is laid
     Some heart once pregnant with celestial fire;
Hands, that the rod of empire might have
          swayed
     Or waked to ecstasy the living lyre.

But Knowledge to their eyes her ample page
     Rich with the spoils of time did ne'er unroll;
Chill Penury repressed their noble rage,
     And froze the genial current of the soul.

Full many a gem of purest ray serene
     The dark unfathomed caves of ocean bear:
Full many a flower is born to blush unseen,
     And waste its sweetness on the desert air.

Some village Hampden that, with dauntless
          breast,
     The little tyrant of his fields withstood,
Some mute inglorious Milton here may
          rest,

Some Cromwell guiltless of his country's
    blood.

The applause of listening senates to command,
    The threats of pain and ruin to despise,
To scatter plenty o'er a smiling land,
    And read their history in a nation's eyes,

Their lot forbade: nor circumscribed alone
    Their growing virtues, but their crimes
        confined;
Forbade to wade through slaughter to a throne,
    And shut the gates of mercy on mankind;

The struggling pangs of conscious truth to
        hide,
    To quench the blushes of ingenuous shame,
Or heap the shrine of Luxury and Pride
    With incense kindled at the Muse's flame.

Far from the madding crowd's ignoble strife,
    Their sober wishes never learned to stray;
Along the cool, sequestered vale of life
    They kept the noiseless tenor of their way.

Yet even these bones from insult to protect
    Some frail memorial still erected nigh,
With uncouth rhymes and shapeless sculpture
        decked,
    Implores the passing tribute of a sigh.

Their name, their years, spelt by the unlettered
    Muse,
  The place of fame and elegy supply:
And many a holy text around she strews,
    That teach the rustic moralist to die.

For who, to dumb Forgetfulness a prey,
    This pleasing anxious being e'er resigned,
Left the warm precincts of the cheerful day,
    Nor cast one longing lingering look behind?

On some fond breast the parting soul relies,
    Some pious drops the closing eye requires;
E'en from the tomb the voice of Nature cries,
    E'en in our ashes live their wonted fires.

For thee, who, mindful of the unhonored dead,
    Dost in these lines their artless tale relate;
If chance, by lonely contemplation led,
    Some kindred spirit shall inquire thy fate —

Haply some hoary-headed swain may say
    "Oft have we seen him at the peep of dawn
Brushing with hasty steps the dews away
    To meet the sun upon the upland lawn.

"There at the foot of yonder nodding beech
    That wreathes its old fantastic roots so high,
His listless length at noontide would he stretch,
    And pore upon the brook that babbles by.

"Hard by yon wood, now smiling as in scorn,
  Muttering his wayward fancies he would
    rove,
Now drooping, woeful-wan, like one forlorn,
  Or crazed with care, or crossed in hopeless
    love.

"One morn I missed him on the 'customed
    hill,
  Along the heath, and near his favorite tree;
Another came; nor yet beside the rill,
  Nor up the lawn, nor at the wood was he:

"The next, with dirges due in sad array,
  Slow through the church-way path we saw
    him borne
Approach and read (for thou canst read) the lay
  Graved on the stone beneath yon aged
    thorn:"

The Epitaph

Here rests his head upon the lap of Earth
  A Youth, to Fortune and to Fame unknown.
Fair Science frowned not on his humble birth,
  And Melancholy marked him for her own.

Large was his bounty, and his soul sincere,
  Heaven did a recompense as largely send:

219

He gave to Misery (all he had) a tear,
He gained from Heaven ('twas all he
wished) a friend.

No farther seek his merits to disclose,
Or draw his frailties from their dread abode,
(There they alike in trembling hope repose,)
The bosom of his Father and his God.

Thomas Gray

Lucy

She dwelt among the untrodden ways
  Beside the springs of Dove,
A Maid whom there were none to praise
  And very few to love:

A violet by a mossy stone
  Half hidden from the eye!
Fair as a star, when only one
  Is shining in the sky.

She lived unknown, and few could know
  When Lucy ceased to be;
But she is in her grave, and, oh,
  The difference to me!

William Wordsworth

'Tis the Last Rose of Summer

'Tis the last rose of Summer,
  Left blooming alone;
All her lovely companions
  Are faded and gone;
No flower of her kindred,
  No rosebud is nigh,
To reflect back her blushes,
  Or give sigh for sigh!

I'll not leave thee, thou lone one,
  To pine on the stem;
Since the lovely are sleeping,
  Go sleep thou with them.
Thus kindly I scatter
  Thy leaves o'er the bed
Where thy mates of the garden
  Lie scentless and dead.

So soon may I follow,
  When friendships decay,
And from Love's shining circle
  The gems drop away!
When true hearts lie withered,
  And fond ones are flown,
Oh! who would inhabit
  This bleak world alone?

Thomas Moore

The Old Familiar Faces

I have had playmates, I have had companions,
In my days of childhood, in my joyful school-
    days;
All, all are gone, the old familiar faces.

I have been laughing, I have been carousing,
Drinking late, sitting late, with my bosom
    cronies;
All, all are gone, the old familiar faces.

I loved a Love once, fairest among women:
Closed are her doors on me, I must not see
    her, —
All, all are gone, the old familiar faces.

I have a friend, a kinder friend has no man,
Like an ingrate, I left my friend abruptly;
Left him, to muse on the old familiar faces.

Ghost-like I paced round the haunts of my
    childhood,
Earth seemed a desert I was bound to traverse,
Seeking to find the old familiar faces.

Friend of my bosom, thou more than a brother,
Why wert not thou born in my father's
    dwelling?
So might we talk of the old familiar faces.

How some they have died, and some they have
    left me,
And some are taken from me; all are departed;
All, all are gone, the old familiar faces.

Charles Lamb

Fare Thee Well!

Fare thee well! and if for ever,
    Still for ever, fare thee well:
    Even though unforgiving, never
    'Gainst thee shall my heart rebel.

Would that breast were bared before thee
    Where thy head so oft hath lain,
While that placid sleep came o'er thee
    Which thou ne'er canst know again!

All my faults perchance thou knowest,
    All my madness none can know;
All my hopes, where'er thou goest,
    Wither, yet with *thee* they go.

Every feeling hath been shaken;
    Pride, which not a world could bow,
Bows to thee, — by thee forsaken,
    Even my soul forsakes me now:

But 'tis done: all words are idle, —

Words from me are vainer still;
  But the thoughts we cannot bridle
    Force their way without the will.

Fare thee well! — thus disunited,
  Torn from every nearer tie,
Seared in heart, and lone, and blighted,
  More than this I scarce can die.
                    George Gordon, Lord Byron

To the Fringed Gentian

Thou blossom bright with autumn dew,
And colored with the heaven's own blue,
That openest when the quiet light
Succeeds the keen and frosty night,

Thou comest not when violets lean
O'er wandering brooks and springs unseen,
Or columbines, in purple dressed,
Nod o'er the ground-bird's hidden nest.

Thou waitest late and com'st alone,
When woods are bare and birds are flown,
And frost and shortening days portend
The aged year is near his end.

Then doth thy sweet and quiet eye

Look through its fringes to the sky,
Blue — blue — as if that sky let fall
A flower from its cerulean wall.

I would that thus, when I shall see
The hour of death draw near to me,
Hope, blossoming within my heart,
May look to heaven as I depart.
                    William Cullen Bryant

The Bridge of Sighs

One more Unfortunate,
    Weary of breath,
Rashly importunate,
    Gone to her death!

Take her up tenderly,
    Lift her with care;
Fashion'd so slenderly,
    Young, and so fair!

Look at her garments
Clinging like cerements;
Whilst the wave constantly
    Drips from her clothing;
Take her up instantly,
    Loving, not loathing.
                    Thomas Hood

Terminus

It is time to be old,
To take in sail: —
The god of bounds,
Who sets to seas a shore,
Come to me in his fatal rounds,
And said: ''No more!
No farther shoot
The broad ambitious branches, and thy root.
Fancy departs: no more invent;
Contract thy firmament
To compass of a tent.
There's not enough for this and that,
Make thy option which of two;
Economize the failing river,
Not the less revere the Giver,
Leave the many and hold the few.
Timely wise accept the terms,
Soften the fall with wary foot;
A little while
Still plan and smile,
And, — fault of novel germs, —
Mature the unfallen fruit.
Curse, if thou wilt, thy sires,
Bad husbands of their fires,
Who, when they gave thee breath,
Failed to bequeath
The needful sinew stark as once,
The baresark marrow to thy bones,

But left a legacy of ebbing veins,
Inconstant heat and nerveless reins, —
Amid the Muses, left thee deaf and dumb,
Amid the gladiators, halt and numb.''

As the bird trims her to the gale,
I trim myself to the storm of time,
I man the rudder, reef the sail,
Obey the voice at eve obeyed at prime:
Lowly faithful, banish fear,
Right onward drive unharmed;
The port, well worth the cruise, is near,
And every wave is charmed.''

Ralph Waldo Emerson

Mezzo Cammin

*(Written at Boppard on the Rhine, August 25,
    1842, just before leaving for home)*
Half of my life is gone, and I have let
    The years slip from me and have not
        fulfilled
    The aspiration of my youth, to build
    Some tower of song with lofty parapet.
Not indolence, nor pleasure, nor the fret
    Of restless passions that would not be stilled,
    But sorrow, and a care that almost killed,
    Kept me from what I may accomplish yet;
Though, half-way up the hill, I see the Past

227

Lying beneath me with its sounds and
  sights, —
A city in the twilight dim and vast,
With smoking roofs, soft bells, and gleaming
  lights, —
And hear above me on the autumnal blast
The cataract of Death far thundering from
  the heights.

                    Henry Wadsworth Longfellow

Memory

My childhood's home I see again,
  And sadden with the view;
And still, as memory crowds my brain,
  There's pleasure in it, too.

O memory! thou midway world
  'Twixt earth and paradise,
Where things decayed and loved ones lost
  In dreamy shadows rise,

And, freed from all that's earthly, vile,
  Seem hallowed, pure and bright,
Like scenes in some enchanted isle
  All bathed in liquid light.

As dusky mountains please the eye

When twilight chases day;
As bugle notes that, passing by,
  In distance die away;

As, leaving some grand waterfall,
  We, lingering, list its roar —
So memory will hallow all
  We've known but know no more.

Near twenty years have passed away
  Since here I bid farewell
To woods and fields, and scenes of play,
  And playmates loved so well.

Where many were, but few remain
  Of old familiar things,
But seeing them to mind again
  The lost and absent brings.

The friends I left that parting day,
  How changed, as time has sped!
Young childhood grown, strong manhood gray;
  And half of all are dead.

I hear the loved survivors tell
  How nought from death could save,
Till every sound appears a knell
  And every spot a grave.

I range the fields with pensive tread,

And pace the hollow rooms,
And feel (companion of the dead)
I'm living in the tombs.
Abraham Lincoln

Annabel Lee

It was many and many a year ago,
   In a kingdom by the sea,
That a maiden there lived whom you may
     know
   By the name of Annabel Lee;
And this maiden she lived with no other
     thought
   Than to love and be loved by me.

I was a child and she was a child,
   In this kingdom by the sea;
But we loved with a love that was more than
     love,
   I and my Annabel Lee;
With a love that the winged seraphs of heaven
   Coveted her and me.

And this was the reason that, long ago,
   In this kingdom by the sea,
A wind blew out of a cloud, chilling
   My beautiful Annabel Lee;

So that her high-born kinsman came
  And bore her away from me,
To shut her up in a sepulcher
  In this kingdom by the sea.

The angels, not half so happy in heaven,
  Went envying her and me.
Yes, that was the reason — as all men know,
  In this kingdom by the sea
That the wind came out of the cloud by night,
  Chilling and killing my Annabel Lee.

But our love it was stronger far than the love
  Of those that were older than we,
  Of many far wiser than we.
And neither the angels in heaven above,
Nor the demons down under the sea,
Can ever dissever my soul from the soul
  Of the beautiful Annabel Lee:

For the moon never beams without bringing me
    dreams
  Of the beautiful Annabel Lee;
And the stars never rise but I feel the bright
    eyes
  Of the beautiful Annabel Lee;
And so, all the night-tide, I lie down by the
    side
Of my darling, my darling, my life, and my
    bride,

In the sepulcher there by the sea,
In her tomb by the sounding sea.

Edgar Allan Poe

Grief

I tell you, hopeless grief is passionless;
   That only men incredulous of despair,
   Half-taught in anguish, through the midnight
     air
Beat upward to God's throne in loud access
Of shrieking and reproach. Full desertness,
   In souls as countries, lieth silent-bare
   Under the blanching, vertical eye-glare
Of the absolute Heavens. Deep-hearted man,
     express
Grief for thy Dead in silence like to death —
   Most like a monumental statue set
In everlasting watch and moveless woe
Till itself crumble to the dust beneath.
   Touch it; the marble eyelids are not wet:
If it could weep, it could arise and go.

Elizabeth Barrett Browning

Crossing the Bar

Sunset and evening star,
   And one clear call for me!

232

And may there be no moaning of the bar,
   When I put out to sea,

But such a tide as moving seems asleep,
   Too full for sound and foam,
When that which drew from out the boundless
     deep
   Turns again home.

Twilight and evening bell,
   And after that the dark!
And may there be no sadness of farewell,
   When I embark;

For though from out our bourne of Time and
     Place
   The flood may bear me far,
I hope to see my Pilot face to face
   When I have crossed the bar.

                   Alfred Tennyson

Tears, Idle Tears

Tears, idle tears, I know not what they
     mean,
Tears from the depth of some divine despair
Rise in the heart, and gather to the eyes,
In looking on the happy autumn-fields,
And thinking of the days that are no more.

Fresh as the first beam glittering on a sail,
That brings our friends up from the
    underworld,
Sad as the last which reddens over one
That sinks with all we love below the verge;
So sad, so fresh, the days that are no more.

Ah, sad and strange as in dark summer
    dawns
The earliest pipe of half-awakened birds
To dying ears, when unto dying eyes
The casement slowly grows a glimmering
    square;
So sad, so strange, the days that are no more.

Dear as remembered kisses after death,
And sweet as those by hopeless fancy feigned
On lips that are for others; deep as love,
Deep as first love, and wild with all regret;
O Death in Life, the days that are no more!

                              Alfred Tennyson

When Lilacs Last in the Dooryard Bloomed

1

When lilacs last in the dooryard bloomed,
And the great star early drooped in the western
  sky in the night,

I mourned, and yet shall mourn with ever-
   returning spring.

Ever-returning spring, trinity sure to me you
   bring,
Lilac blooming perennial and drooping star in
   the west,
And thought of him I love.

2

O powerful western fallen star!
O shades of night — O moody, tearful night!
O great star disappeared — O the black murk
   that hides the star!
O cruel hands that hold me powerless — O
   helpless soul of me!
O harsh surrounding cloud that will not free
   my soul.

3

In the dooryard fronting an old farmhouse near
   the whitewashed palings,
Stand the lilac bush tall-growing with heart-
   shaped leaves of rich green,
With many a pointed blossom rising delicate,
   with the perfume strong I love,
With every leaf a miracle — and from this
   bush in the dooryard,
With delicate-colored blossoms and heart-
   shaped leaves of rich green,
A sprig with its flower I break.

4

In the swamp in secluded recesses,
A shy and hidden bird is warbling a song.

Solitary the thrush,
The hermit withdrawn to himself, avoiding the
 settlements,
Sings by himself a song.

Song of the bleeding throat,
Death's outlet song of life (for well dear
 brother I know,
If thou wast not granted to sing thou wouldst
 surely die).

5

Over the breast of the spring, the land, amid
 cities,
Amid lanes and through old woods, where
 lately the violets peeped from the ground,
 spotting the gray debris,
Amid the grass in the fields each side of the
 lanes, passing the endless grass,
Passing the yellow-speared wheat, every grain
 from its shroud in the dark-brown fields
 uprisen,
Passing the apple-tree blows of white and pink
 in the orchards,
Carrying a corpse to where it shall rest in the
 grave,

Night and day journeys a coffin.

6

Coffin that passes through lanes and streets,
Through day and night with the great cloud
    darkening the land,
With the pomp of the inlooped flags with the
    cities draped in black,
With the show of the States themselves as of
    crape-veiled women standing,
With processions long and winding and the
    flambeaus of the night,
With the countless torches lit, with the silent
    sea of faces and the unbared heads,
With the waiting depot, the arriving coffin, and
    the somber faces,
With dirges through the night, with the
    thousand voices rising strong and solemn,
With all the mournful voices of the dirges
    poured around the coffin,
The dim-lit churches and the shuddering organs
    — where amid these you journey,
With the tolling tolling bells' perpetual clang,
Here, coffin that slowly passes,
I give you my sprig of lilac.

7

(Nor for you, for one alone,
Blossoms and branches green to coffins all I
    bring,

237

For fresh as the morning, thus would I chant a
  song for you
O sane and sacred death.
All over bouquets of roses,
O death, I cover you over with roses and early
  lilies,
But mostly and now the lilac that blooms the
  first,
Copious I break, I break the sprigs from the
  bushes,
With loaded arms I come, pouring for you,
For you and the coffins all of you O death.)

8

O western orb sailing the heaven,
Now I know what you must have meant as a
  month since I walked,
As I walked in silence the transparent shadowy
  night,
As I saw you had something to tell as you
  bent to me night after night,
As you drooped from the sky low down as if
  to my side (while the other stars all looked
  on),
As we wandered together the solemn night (for
  something I know not what kept me from
  sleep),
As the night advanced, and I saw on the rim of
  the west how full you were of woe,
As I stood on the rising ground in the breeze in

the cool transparent night,
As I watched where you passed and was lost in
the netherward black of the night,
As my soul in its trouble dissatisfied sank, as
where you sad orb,
Concluded, dropped in the night, and was
gone.

9

Sing on there in the swamp,
O singer bashful and tender, I hear your notes,
I hear your call,
I hear, I come presently, I understand you,
But a moment I linger, for the lustrous star has
detained me,
The star my departing comrade holds and
detains me.

10

O how shall I warble myself for the dead one
there I loved?
And how shall I deck my song for the large
sweet soul that has gone?
And what shall my perfume be for the grave of
him I love?
Sea winds blown from east and west,
Blown from the Eastern sea and blown from
the Western sea, till there on the prairies
meeting,
These and with these and the breath of

my chant,
I'll perfume the grave of him I love.

11

O what shall I hang on the chamber walls?
And what shall the pictures be that I hang on
the walls,
To adorn the burial house of him I love?
Pictures of growing spring and farms and
homes,
With the Fourth-month eve at sundown, and
the gray smoke lucid and bright,
With floods of the yellow gold of the
gorgeous, indolent, sinking sun, burning,
expanding the air
With the fresh sweet herbage underfoot, and
the pale green leaves of the trees prolific,
In the distance the flowing glaze, the breast of
the river, with a wind dapple here and there,
With ranging hills on the banks, with many a
line against the sky, and shadows,
And the city at hand with dwellings so dense,
and stacks of chimneys,
And all the scenes of life and the workshops,
and the workmen homeward returning.

12

Lo, body and soul — this land,
My own Manhattan with spires, and the
sparkling and hurrying tides, and the ships,

The varied and ample land, the South and the
   North in the light, Ohio's shores and
   flashing Missouri,
And ever the far-spreading prairies covered
   with grass and corn.
Lo, the most excellent sun so calm and
   haughty,
The violet and purple morn with just-felt
   breezes,
The gentle soft-born measureless light,
The miracle spreading bathing all, the fulfilled
   noon,
The coming eve delicious, the welcome night
   and the stars,
Over my cities shining all, enveloping man and
   land.

13

Sing on, sing on you gray-brown bird,
Sing from the swamps, and recesses, pour your
   chant from the bushes,
Limitless out of the dusk, out of the cedars and
   pines.
Sing on dearest brother, warble your reedy
   song,
Loud human song, with voice of uttermost
   woe.
O liquid and free and tender!
O wild and loose to my soul — O wondrous
   singer!

You only I hear — yet the star holds me (but
will soon depart),
Yet the lilac with mastering odor holds me.

14

Now while I sat in the day and looked forth,
In the close of the day with its light and the
fields of spring, and the farmers preparing
their crops,
In the large unconscious scenery of my land
with its lakes and forests,
In the heavenly aerial beauty (after the
perturbed winds and the storms),
Under the arching heavens of the afternoon
swift passing, and the voices of children and
women,
The many-moving sea tides, and I saw the
ships how they sailed,
And the summer approaching with richness,
and the fields all busy with labor,
And the infinite separate houses, how they all
went on, each with its meals and minutia of
daily usages,
And the streets how their throbbings throbbed,
and the cities pent — lo, then and there,
Falling upon them all and among them all,
enveloping me with the rest,
Appeared the cloud, appeared the long black
trail,
And I knew death, its thought, and the sacred

knowledge of death.

Then with the knowledge of death as walking
    one side of me,
And the thought of death close-walking the
    other side of me,
And in the middle as with companions, and as
    holding the hands of companions,
I fled forth to the hiding receiving night that
    talks not,
Down to the shores of the water the path by
    the swamp in the dimness,
To the solemn shadowy cedars and ghostly
    pines so still.
And the singer so shy to the rest received me,
The gray-brown bird I know received us
    comrades three,
And he sang the carol of death, and a verse for
    him I love.
From deep secluded recesses
From the fragrant cedars and the ghostly pines
    so still,
Came the carol of the bird.
And the charm of the carol rapt me,
As I held as if by their hands my comrades in
    the night,
And the voice of my spirit tallied the song of
    the bird.

Come lovely and soothing death,
Undulate round the world, serenely arriving,
   arriving,
In the day, in the night, to all, to each,
Sooner or later delicate death.
Praised be the fathomless universe,
For life and joy, and for objects and
   knowledge curious,
And for love, sweet love — but praise! praise!
   praise!
For the sure-enwinding arms of cool-enfolding
   death.
Dark mother always gliding near with soft feet,
Have none chanted for thee a chant of fullest
   welcome?
Then I chant it for thee, I glorify thee above
   all,
I bring thee a song that when thou must indeed
   come, come unfalteringly.
Approach strong deliveress,
When it is so, when thou hast taken them I
   joyously sing the dead,
Lost in the loving floating ocean of thee,
Laved in the flood of thy bliss O death.
From me to thee glad serenades,
Dances for thee I propose saluting thee,
   adornments and feastings for thee,
And the sights of the open landscape and the
   high-spread sky are fitting,
And life and the fields, and the huge and

thoughtful night.
The night in silence under many a star,
The ocean shore and the husky whispering
wave whose voice I know,
And the soul turning to thee O vast and well-
veiled death,
And the body gratefully nestling close to thee.
Over the treetops I float thee a song,
Over the rising and sinking waves, over the
myriad fields and the prairies wide,
Over the dense-packed cities all and the
teeming wharves and ways,
I float this carol with joy, with joy to thee O
death.

15

To the tally of my soul,
Loud and strong kept up the gray-brown bird,
With pure deliberate notes spreading filling the
night.
Loud in the pines and cedars dim,
Clear in the freshness moist and the swamp
perfume,
And I with my comrades there in the night.
While my sight that was bound in my eyes
unclosed,
As to long panoramas of visions.
And I saw askant the armies,
I saw as in noiseless dreams hundreds of battle
flags,

Borne through the smoke of the battles and
     pierced with missiles I saw them,
And carried hither and yon through the smoke,
     and torn and bloody,
And at last but a few shreds left on the staffs
     (and all in silence),
And the staffs all splintered and broken.
I saw battle corpses, myriads of them,
And the white skeletons of young men, I saw
     them,
I saw the debris and debris of all the slain
     soldiers of the war,
But I saw they were not as was thought,
They themselves were fully at rest, they
     suffered not,
The living remained and suffered, the mother
     suffered,
And the wife and the child and the musing
     comrade suffered,
And the armies that remained suffered.

16

Passing the visions, passing the night,
Passing, unloosing the hold of my comrades'
     hands,
Passing the song of the hermit bird and the
     tallying song of my soul,
Victorious song, death's outlet song, yet
     varying ever-altering song,
As low and wailing, yet clear the notes, rising

and falling, flooding the night,
Sadly sinking and fainting, as warning and
 warning, and yet again bursting with joy,
Covering the earth and filling the spread of the
 heaven,
As that powerful psalm in the night I heard
 from recesses,
Passing, I leave thee lilac with heart-shaped
 leaves,
I leave thee there in the dooryard, blooming,
 returning with spring.
I cease from my song for thee,
From my gaze on thee in the west, fronting the
 west, communing with thee,
O comrade lustrous with silver face in the
 night.

Yet each to keep and all, retrievements out of
 the night,
The song, the wondrous chant of the gray-
 brown bird,
And the tallying chant, the echo aroused in my
 soul,
With lustrous and drooping star with the
 countenance full of woe,
With the holders holding my hand nearing the
 call of the bird,
Comrades mine and I in the midst, and their
 memory ever to keep, for the dead I loved
 so well,

For the sweetest, wisest soul of all my days
  and lands — and this for his dear sake,
Lilac and star and bird twined with the chant
  of my soul,
There in the fragrant pines and the cedars dusk
  and dim.

Walt Whitman

Song

When I am dead, my dearest,
Sing no sad songs for me;
Plant thou no roses at my head,
Nor shady cypress-tree:
Be the green grass above me
With showers and dewdrops wet;
And if thou wilt, remember,
And if thou wilt, forget.

I shall not see the shadows,
I shall not feel the rain;
I shall not hear the nightingale
Sing on, as if in pain:
And dreaming through the twilight
That doth not rise nor set,
Haply I may remember,
And haply may forget.

Christina Georgina Rosetti

Because I Could Not Stop for Death

Because I could not stop for Death —
He kindly stopped for me —
The Carriage held but just Ourselves —
And Immortality.

We slowly drove — He knew no haste
And I had put away
My labor and my leisure too,
For His Civility —

We passed the School, where Children strove
At Recess — in the Ring —
We passed the Fields of Gazing Grain —
We passed the Setting Sun —

Or rather — He passed Us —
The Dews drew quivering and chill —
For only Gossamer, my Gown —
My Tippet — only Tulle —

We paused before a House that seemed
A Swelling of the Ground —
The Roof was scarcely visible —
The Cornice — in the Ground —

Since then — 'tis Centuries — and yet
Feels shorter than the Day

I first surmised the Horses' Heads
Were toward Eternity —

Emily Dickinson

The Bustle in a House

The Bustle in a House
The Morning after Death
Is solemnest of industries
Enacted upon Earth —

The Sweeping up the Heart
And putting Love away
We shall not want to use again
Until Eternity.

Emily Dickinson

I've Seen a Dying Eye

I've seen a Dying Eye
Run round and round a Room —
In search of Something — as it seemed —
Then Cloudier become —
And then — obscure with Fog —
And then — be soldered down
Without disclosing what it be
'Twere blessed to have seen —

Emily Dickinson

Requiem

Under the wide and starry sky
Dig the grave and let me lie.
Glad did I live and gladly die,
    And I laid me down with a will.

This be the verse you grave for me:
Here he lies where he longed to be;
Home is the sailor, home from sea,
    And the hunter home from the hill.
                    Robert Louis Stevenson

Bachelor Hall

It seems like a dream — that sweet wooing of
    old —
Like a legend of fairies on pages of gold —
Too soon the sweet story of loving was closed,
Too rudely awakened the soul that reposed;
I kissed the white lips that lay under the pall,
And crept back to you, lonely Bachelor Hall.

Mine eyes have grown dim and my hair has
    turned white,
But my heart beats as warmly and gaily tonight
As in days that are gone and years that are
    fled —

Though I fill up my flagon and drink to the
   dead;
For over my senses sweet memories fall,
And the dead is come back to old Bachelor
   Hall.

I see her fair face through a vapor of tears,
And her sweet voice comes back o'er the
   desert of years,
And I hear, oh, so gently, the promises she
   spoke,
And a soft spirit hand soothes the heart that is
   broke;
So I fill up the flagon, and drink — that is
   all —
To the dead and the dying of Bachelor Hall.
                                    Eugene Field

Out of the Hitherwhere

Out of the hitherwhere into the yon —
The land that the Lord's love rests upon,
Where one may rely on the friends he meets,
And the smiles that greet him along the streets,
Where the mother that left you years ago
Will lift the hands that were folded so,
And put them about you, with all the love
And tenderness you are dreaming of.

Out of the hitherwhere into the yon —
Where all the friends of your youth have
     gone —
Where the old schoolmate who laughed with
     you
Will laugh again as he used to do,
Running to meet you, with such a face
As lights like a moon the wondrous place
Where God is living, and glad to live
Since He is the Master and may forgive.

Out of the hitherwhere into the yon —
Stay the hopes we are leaning on —
You, Divine, with Your merciful eyes
Looking down from far-away skies,
Smile upon us and reach and take
Our worn souls Home for the old home's
     sake —
And so, Amen — for our all seems gone
Out of the hitherwhere into the yon.

James Whitcomb Riley

He Is Not Dead

I cannot say, and I will not say
That he is dead. He is just away.
With a cheery smile, and a wave of the hand,
He has wandered into an unknown land
And left us dreaming how very fair

It needs must be, since he lingers there.
And you — oh, you, who the wildest yearn
For an old-time step, and the glad return,
Think of him faring on, as dear
In the love of There as the love of Here.
Think of him still as the same. I say,
He is not dead — he is just away.

James Whitcomb Riley

And You As Well Must Die, Beloved Dust

And you as well must die, beloved dust,
And all your beauty stand you in no stead;
This flawless, vital hand, this perfect head,
This body of flame and steel, before the gust
Of Death, or under his autumnal frost,
Shall be as any leaf, be no less dead
Than the first leaf that fell, — this wonder
   fled,
Altered, estranged, disintegrated, lost.
Nor shall my love avail you in your hour.
In spite of all my love, you will arise
Upon that day and wander down the air
Obscurely as the unattended flower,
It mattering not how beautiful you were,
Or how beloved above all else that dies.

Edna St. Vincent Millay

254

Fire and Ice

Some say the world will end in fire,
Some say in ice.
From what I've tasted of desire
I hold with those who favor fire.
But if it had to perish twice,
I think I know enough of hate
To say that for destruction ice
Is also great
And would suffice.

Robert Frost

Patriotism
and War

To Lucasta, Going to the Wars

Tell me not, Sweet, I am unkind,
 That from the nunnery
Of thy chaste breast and quiet mind
 To war and arms I fly.

True, a new mistress now I chase,
 The first foe in the field;
And with a stronger faith embrace
 A sword, a horse, a shield.

Yet this inconstancy is such
 As thou too shalt adore;
I could not love thee, Dear, so much,
 Loved I not Honor more.
                          Richard Lovelace

The Battle of Blenheim

(August 13, 1704)

It was a summer evening;
 Old Kaspar's work was done,
And he before his cottage door

Was sitting in the sun;
And by him sported on the green
His little grandchild, Wilhelmine.

She saw her brother Peterkin
    Roll something large and round,
That he beside the rivulet,
    In playing there, had found:
She ran to ask what he had found,
That was so large and smooth and round.

Old Kaspar took it from the boy,
    Who stood expectant by;
And then the old man shook his head,
    And with a natural sigh,
" 'Tis some poor fellow's skull," said he,
"Who fell in the great victory.

"I find them in my garden,
    For there's many here about;
And often, when I go to plough,
    The ploughshare turns them out;
For many thousand men," said he,
"Were slain in that great victory."

"Now tell us what 'twas all about,"
    Young Peterkin, he cries;
And little Wilhelmine looks up
    With wonder-waiting eyes;
"Now tell us all about the war,

And what they fought each other for."

"It was the English," Kaspar cried,
    "Who put the French to rout;
But what they fought each other for
    I could not well make out;
But everybody said," quoth he,
"That 'twas a famous victory.

"My father lived at Blenheim then,
    Yon little stream hard by;
They burned his dwelling to the ground,
    And he was forced to fly;
So with his wife and child he fled,
Nor had he where to rest his head.

"With fire and sword the country round
    Was wasted far and wide,
And many a childing mother then,
    And new-born baby, died;
But things like that, you know, must be
At every famous victory.

"They say it was a shocking sight
    After the field was won;
For many thousand bodies here
    Lay rotting in the sun:
But things like that, you know, must be
After a famous victory.

"Great praise the Duke of Marlborough won
  And our good Prince Eugene."
"Why, 'twas a very wicked thing!"
  Said little Wilhelmine.
"Nay, nay, my little girl," quoth he,
"It was a famous victory.

"And everybody praised the Duke,
  Who this great fight did win."
"But what good came of it at last?"
  Quoth little Peterkin.
"Why, that I cannot tell," said he;
"But 'twas a famous victory."

Robert Southey

Breathes There the Man

Breathes there the man with soul so dead
Who never to himself hath said,
  This is my own, my native land!
Whose heart hath ne'er within him burned,
As home his footsteps he hath turned
  From wandering on a foreign strand?
If such there breathe, go, mark him well;
For him no minstrel raptures swell;
High though his titles, proud his name,
Boundless his wealth as wish can claim,
Despite those titles, power, and pelf,
The wretch, concentred all in self,

Living, shall forefeit fair renown,
And, doubly dying, shall go down
To the vile dust from whence he sprung,
Unwept, unhonored, and unsung.
(From *"The Lay of the Last Minstrel,"*
Canto VI.)
Sir Walter Scott

The Battle-Field

Once this soft turf, this rivulet's sands,
   Were trampled by a hurrying crowd,
And fiery hearts and armed hands
   Encountered in the battle-cloud.

Ah! never shall the land forget
   How gushed the life-blood of her brave —
Gushed, warm with hope and courage yet,
   Upon the soil they fought to save.

Now all is calm, and fresh, and still;
   Alone the chirp of flitting bird,
And talk of children on the hill,
   And bell of wandering kine, are heard.

No solemn host goes trailing by
   The black-mouthed gun and staggerng wain;
Men start not at the battle-cry,
   Oh, be it never heard again!

Soon rested those who fought; but thou
    Who minglest in the harder strife
For truths which men receive not now,
    Thy warfare only ends with life.

A friendless warfare! lingering long
    Through weary day and weary year;
A wild and many-weaponed throng
    Hang on thy front, and flank, and rear.
Yet nerve thy spirit to the proof,
    And blench not at thy chosen lot,
The timid good may stand aloof,
    The sage may frown — yet faint thou not.

Nor heed the shaft too surely cast,
    The foul and hissing bolt of scorn;
For with thy side shall dwell, at last,
    The victory of endurance born.

Truth, crushed to earth, shall rise again;
    Th' eternal years of God are hers;
But Error, wounded, writhes in pain,
    And dies among his worshippers.

Yea, though thou lie upon the dust,
    When they who helped thee flee in fear,
Die full of hope and manly trust,
    Like those who fell in battle here.

Another hand thy sword shall wield,

Another hand the standard wave,
Till from the trumpet's mouth is pealed
The blast of triumph o'er thy grave.
William Cullen Bryant

In an Age of Fops and Toys

In an age of fops and toys,
Wanting wisdom, void of right,
Who shall nerve heroic boys
To hazard all in Freedom's fight, —
Break sharply off their jolly games,
Forsake their comrades gay
And quit proud homes and youthful dames
For famine, toil and fray?
Yet on the nimble air benign
Speed nimbler messages,
That waft the breath of grace divine
To hearts in sloth and ease.
So nigh is grandeur to our dust,
So near is God to man,
When Duty whispers low, *Thou must,*
The youth replies, *I can.*

(From *Voluntaries*)
Ralph Waldo Emerson

The Charge of the Light Brigade

Half a league, half a league,
  Half a league onward,
All in the valley of Death
  Rode the six hundred.
"Forward, the Light Brigade!
Charge for the guns," he said:
Into the valley of Death
  Rode the six hundred.
"Forward, the Light Brigade!"
Was there a man dismay'd?

Not tho' the soldier knew
  Someone had blunder'd:
Theirs not to make reply,
Theirs not to reason why,
Theirs but to do and die:
Into the valley of Death
  Rode the six hundred.

Cannon to right of them,
Cannon to left of them,
Cannon in front of them
  Volley'd and thunder'd;
Storm'd at with shot and shell,
Boldly they rode and well,
Into the jaws of Death,

Into the mouth of Hell
  Rode the six hundred.

Flash'd all their sabers bare,
Flash'd as they turn'd in air
Sabring the gunners there,
Charging an army, while
  All the world wonder'd:
Plung'd in the battery-smoke
Right thro' the line they broke;
Cossack and Russian
Reel'd from the saber-stroke
  Shatter'd and sunder'd.
Then they rode back, but not,
  Not the six hundred.

Cannon to right of them,
Cannon to left of them,
Cannon behind them
  Volley'd and thunder'd;
Storm'd at with shot and shell,
While horse and hero fell,
They that had fought so well
Came thro' the jaws of Death,
Back from the mouth of Hell,
All that was left of them,
  Left of six hundred.
When can their glory fade?
O the wild charge they made!
  All the world wonder'd.

Honor the charge they made!
Honor the Light Brigade,
Noble six hundred!
Alfred Tennyson

Barbara Frietchie

Up from the meadows rich with corn,
Clear in the cool September morn,

The clustered spires of Frederick stand
Green-walled by the hills of Maryland.

Round about them orchards sweep,
Apple and peach tree fruited deep,

Fair as the garden of the Lord
To the eyes of the famished rebel horde,

On that pleasant morn of the early fall
When Lee marched over the mountain-wall;

Over the mountains winding down,
Horse and foot, into Frederick town,

Forty flags with their silver stars,
Forty flags with their crimson bars,

Flapped in the morning wind: the sun

Of noon looked down, and saw not one.

Up rose old Barbara Frietchie then,
Bowed with her fourscore years and ten;

Bravest of all in Frederick town,
She took up the flag the men hauled down;

In her attic window the staff she set,
To show that one heart was loyal yet.

Up the street came the rebel tread,
Stonewall Jackson riding ahead.

Under his slouched hat left and right
He glanced; the old flag met his sight.

''Halt!'' — the dust-brown ranks stood fast.
''Fire!'' — out blazed the rifle-blast.

It shivered the window, pane and sash;
It rent the banner with seam and gash.

Quick as it fell, from the broken staff
Dame Barbara snatched the silken scarf.

She leaned far out on the window-sill,
And shook it forth with a royal will.

''Shoot, if you must, this old gray head,

But spare your country's flag," she said.

A shade of sadness, a blush of shame,
Over the face of the leader came;

The nobler nature within him stirred
To life at that woman's deed and word;

"Who touches a hair of yon gray head
Dies like a dog! March on!" he said.

All day long through Frederick street
Sounded the tread of marching feet:

All day long that free flag tossed
Over the heads of the rebel host.

Ever its torn folds rose and fell
On the loyal winds that loved it well;

And through the hill-gaps sunset light
Shone over it with a warm good-night.

Barbara Frietchie's work is o'er,
And the Rebel rides on his raids no more.

Honor to her! and let a tear
Fall, for her sake, on Stonewall's bier.

Over Barbara Frietchie's grave,

Flag of Freedom and Union, wave!

Peace and order and beauty draw
Round thy symbol of light and law;

And ever the stars above look down
On thy stars below in Frederick town!
John Greenleaf Whittier

Malvern Hill

(July 1862)

Ye elms that wave on Malvern Hill
   In prime of morn and May,
Recall ye how McClellan's men
     Here stood at bay?
While deep within yon forest dim
   Our rigid comrades lay —
Some with the cartridge in their mouth,
Others with fixed arms lifted South —
     Invoking so
The cypress glades? Ah wilds of woe!

The spires of Richmond, late beheld
   Through rifts in musket-haze,
Were closed from view in clouds of dust
     On leaf-walled ways,
Where streamed our wagons in caravan;

And the Seven Nights and Days
Of march and fast, retreat and fight,
Pinched our grimed faces to ghastly plight —
    Does the elm wood
Recall the haggard beards of blood?

The battle-smoked flag, with stars eclipsed,
    We followed (it never fell!) —
In silence husbanded our strength —
    Received their yell;
Till on this slope we patient turned
    With cannon ordered well;
Reverse we proved was not defeat;
But ah, the sod what thousands meet! —
    Does Malvern Wood
Bethink itself, and muse and brood?

    We elms of Malvern Hill
      Remember every thing;
    But sap the twig will fill:
    Wag the world how it will,
      Leaves must be green in Spring
          Herman Melville

Old Ironsides

Ay, tear her tattered ensign down!
    Long has it waved on high,
And many an eye has danced to see

That banner in the sky;
Beneath it rung the battle shout,
  And burst the cannon's roar; —
The meteor of the ocean air
  Shall sweep the clouds no more.

Her deck, once red with heroes' blood,
  Where knelt the vanquished foe,
When winds were hurrying o'er the flood,
  And waves were white below,
No more shall feel the victor's tread,
  Or know the conquered knee; —
The harpies of the shore shall pluck
  The eagle of the sea!

Oh, better that her shattered hulk
  Should sink beneath the wave;
Her thunders shook the mighty deep,
  And there should be her grave;
Nail to the mast her holy flag,
  Set every threadbare sail,
And give her to the god of storms,
The lightning and the gale!
                    Oliver Wendell Holmes

Beat! Beat! Drums!

Beat! beat! drums! — blow! bugles! blow!
Through the windows — through doors —

burst like a ruthless force,
Into the solemn church, and scatter the
  congregation,
Into the school where the scholar is studying;
Leave not the bridegroom quiet — no
  happiness must he have now with his bride,
Or the peaceful farmer any peace, ploughing
  his field or gathering his grain,
So fierce you whirr and pound you drums —
  so shrill you bugles blow.

Beat! beat! drums! — blow! bugles! blow!
Over the traffic of cities — over the rumble of
  wheels in the streets;
Are beds prepared for sleepers at night in the
  houses? no sleepers must sleep in those
  beds,
No bargainers' bargains by day — no brokers
  or speculators — would they continue?
Would the talkers be talking? would the singer
  attempt to sing?
Would the lawyer rise in the court to state his
  case before the judge?
Then rattle quicker, heavier drums — you
  bugles wilder blow.

Beat! beat! drums! — blow! bugles! blow!
Make no parley — stop for no expostulation,
Mind not the timid — mind not the weeper or
  prayer,

Mind not the old man beseeching the young
    man,
Let not the child's voice be heard, nor the
    mother's entreaties,
Make even the trestles to shake the dead where
    they lie awaiting the hearses,
So strong you thump O terrible drums — so
    loud you bugles blow.

Walt Whitman

O Captain! My Captain!

O Captain! my Captain! our fearful trip is
       done,
The ship has weathered every rack, the prize
       we sought is won,
The port is near, the bells I hear, the people all
       exulting,
While follow eyes the steady keel, the vessel
       grim and daring
  But O heart! heart! heart!
    O the bleeding drops of red,
  Where on the deck my Captain lies,
    Fallen cold and dead.

O Captain! my Captain! rise up and hear the
       bells;
Rise up — for you the flag is flung — for you
       the bugle trills,

For you bouquets and ribboned wreaths — for
       you the shores a-crowding,
For you they call, the swaying mass, their
       eager faces turning;
    Here Captain! dear father!
      This arm beneath your head!
    It is some dream that on the deck
      You've fallen cold and dead.

My Captain does not answer, his lips are pale
       and still,
My father does not feel my arm, he has no
       pulse nor will,
The ship is anchored safe and sound, its
       voyage closed and done,
From fearful trip the victor ship comes in with
       object won;
    Exult O shores, and ring O bells!
      But I with mournful tread,
    Walk the deck my Captain lies,
      Fallen cold and dead.

Walt Whitman

I Hear America Singing

I hear America singing, the varied carols I
  hear,
Those of mechanics, each one singing his as it
  should be blithe and strong,

The carpenter singing his as he measures his
  plank or beam,
The mason singing his as he makes ready for
  work, or leaves off work,
The boatman singing what belongs to him in
  his boat, the deckhand singing on the
  steamboat deck,
The shoemaker singing as he sits on his bench,
  the hatter singing as he stands,
The wood-cutter's song, the plowboy's on his
  way in the morning, or at noon intermission
  or at sundown,
The delicious singing of the mother, or of the
  young wife at work, or of the girl sewing or
  washing,
Each singing what belongs to him or her and to
  none else,
The day what belongs to the day — at night
  the party of young fellows, robust, friendly,
Singing with open mouths their strong
  melodious songs.

Walt Whitman

The New Colossus

Not like the brazen giant of Greek fame,
With conquering limbs astride from land to
  land;

Here at our sea-washed, sunset gates shall
  stand
A mighty woman with a torch, whose flame
Is the imprisoned lightning, and her name
Mother of Exiles. From her beacon-hand
Glows world-wide welcome; her mild eyes
  command
The air-bridged harbor that twin cities frame.
"Keep, ancient lands, your storied pomp!"
  cries she
With silent lips. "Give me your tired, your
  poor,
Your huddled masses yearning to breathe free,
The wretched refuse of your teeming shore.
Send these, the homeless, tempest-tost to me,
I lift my lamp beside the golden door!"

Emma Lazarus

Boots

(Infantry Columns)

We're foot — slog — slog — slog — sloggin'
  over Africa,
Foot — foot — foot — foot — sloggin' over
  Africa,
(Boots — boots — boots — boots — movin'
  up and down again!)
    There's no discharge in the war!

Seven — six — eleven — five — nine-
   an'-twenty mile to-day —
Four — eleven — seventeen — thirty-two the
   day before —
(Boots — boots — boots — boots — movin'
   up and down again!)
     There's no discharge in the war!

Don't — don't — don't — don't — look at
   what's in front of you.
(Boots — boots — boots — boots — movin'
   up an' down again),
Men — men — men — men — men go mad
   with watchin' 'em,
     An' there's no discharge in the war!

Try — try — try — try — to think o'
   something different —
Oh — my — God — keep — me from goin'
   lunatic!
(Boots — boots — boots — boots — movin'
   up an' down again!)
     There's no discharge in the war!

Count — count — count — count — the
   bullets in the bandoliers.
If — your — eyes — drop — they will get
   atop o' you.
(Boots — boots — boots — boots — movin'
   up and down again) —
     There's no discharge in the war!

We — can — stick — out —'unger, thirst, an'
    weariness,
But — not — not — not — not the chronic
    sight of 'em —
Boots — boots — boots — boots — movin'
    up an' down again,
      An' there's no discharge in the war!

Tain't — so — bad — by — day because o'
    company,
But — night — brings — long — strings — o'
    forty thousand million
Boots — boots — boots — boots — movin'
    up an' down again.
      There's no discharge in the war!

I — 'ave — marched — six — weeks in 'Ell
    an' certify
It — is — not — fire — devils — dark or
    anything,
But boots — boots — boots — boots —
    movin' up an' down again,
      An' there's no discharge in the war!
                Rudyard Kipling

Independence Bell — July 4, 1776

There was a tumult in the city
In the quaint old Quaker town,
And the streets were rife with people

Pacing restless up and down —
People gathering at corners,
Where they whispered each to each,
And the sweat stood on their temples
With the earnestness of speech.

As the bleak Atlantic currents
Lash the wild Newfoundland shore,
So they beat against the State House,
So they surged against the door;
And the mingling of their voices
Made the harmony profound,
Till the quiet street of Chestnut
Was all turbulent with sound.

"Will they do it?" "Dare they do it?"
"Who is speaking?" "What's the news?"
"What of Adams?" "What of Sherman?"
"Oh, God grant they won't refuse!"
"Make some way there!" "Let me nearer!"
"I am stifling!" "Stifle then!
When a nation's life's at hazard,
We've no time to think of men!"

So they surged against the State House,
While all solemnly inside,
Sat the Continental Congress,
Truth and reason for their guide,
O'er a simple scroll debating,
Which, though simple it might be,

Yet should shake the cliffs of England
With the thunders of the free.

Far aloft in that high steeple
Sat the bellman, old and gray,
He was weary of the tyrant
And his iron-sceptered sway;
So he sat, with one hand ready
On the clapper of the bell,
When his eye could catch the signal,
The long-expected news to tell.

See! See! The dense crowd quivers
Through all its lengthy line,
As the boy beside the portal
Hastens forth to give the sign!
With his little hands uplifted,
Breezes dallying with his hair,
Hark! with deep, clear intonation,
Breaks his young voice on the air.

Hushed the people's swelling murmur,
Whilst the boy crys joyously;
"Ring!" he shouts, "Ring! Grandpapa,
Ring! oh, ring for Liberty!"
Quickly, at the given signal
The old bellman lifts his hand,
Forth he sends the good news, making
Iron music through the land.

How they shouted! What rejoicing!
How the old bell shook the air,
Till the clang of freedom ruffled,
The calmly gliding Delaware!
How the bonfires and the torches
Lighted up the night's repose,
And from the flames, like fabled Phoenix,
Our glorious liberty arose!

That old State House bell is silent,
Hushed is now its clamorous tongue;
But the spirit it awakened
Still is living — ever young;
And when we greet the smiling sunlight
On the fourth of each July,
We will ne'er forget the bellman
Who, betwixt the earth and sky,
Rung out, loudly, "Independence";
Which, please God, shall never die!

Unknown

Do Not Weep, Maiden, for War Is Kind

Do not weep, maiden, for war is kind.
Because your lover threw wild hands toward
    the sky
And the affrighted steed ran on alone,
Do not weep.
War is kind.

283

Hoarse, booming drums of the regiment,
Little souls who thirst for fight —
These men were born to drill and die.
The unexplained glory flies above them;
Great is the battle-god, great — and his
    kingdom
A field where a thousand corpses lie.

Do not weep, babe, for war is kind.
Because your father tumbled in the yellow
    trenches,
Raged at his breast, gulped and died,
Do not weep.
War is kind.

Swift-blazing flag of the regiment,
Eagle with crest of red and gold,
These men were born to drill and die.
Point for them the virtue of slaughter,
Make plain to them the excellence of killing,
And a field where a thousand corpses lie.

Mother whose heart hung humble as a button
On the bright splendid shroud of your son,
Do not weep.
War is kind.

(From *War Is Kind*)
Stephen Crane

In Flanders Fields

In Flanders fields the poppies blow
Between the crosses, row on row,
    That mark our place; and in the sky
    The larks, still bravely singing, fly
Scarce heard amid the guns below.

We are the Dead. Short days ago
We lived, felt dawn, saw sunset glow,
    Loved and were loved, and now we lie
    In Flanders fields.

Take up our quarrel with the foe:
To you from failing hands we throw
    The torch; be yours to hold it high.
    If ye break faith with us who die
We shall not sleep, though poppies grow
    In Flanders fields.

John McCrae

The Soldier

If I should die, think only this of me:
That there's some corner of a foreign field
That is forever England. There shall be
In that rich earth a richer dust concealed;
A dust whom England bore, shaped, made
   aware,
Gave, once, her flowers to love, her ways to
   roam;
A body of England's, breathing English air,
Washed by the rivers, blest by suns of home.
And think, this heart, all evil shed away,
A pulse in the eternal mind, no less
Gives somewhere back the thoughts by
   England given;
Her sights and sounds; dreams happy as her
   day;
And laughter, learnt of friends; and gentleness,
In hearts at peace, under an English heaven.

(From *1914*)
Rupert Brooke

The Unknown Soldier

There's a graveyard near the White House
   Where the Unknown Soldier lies,
And the flowers there are sprinkled
   With the tears from mother's eyes.

I stood there not so long ago
   With roses for the brave,
And suddenly I heard a voice
   Speak from out the grave:

"I am the Unknown Soldier,"
   The spirit voice began,
"And I think I have the right
   To ask some questions man to man.

"Are my buddies taken care of?
   Was their victory so sweet?
Is that big reward you offered
   Selling pencils on the street?

"Did they really win the freedom
   They battled to achieve?
Do you still respect that Croix de Guerre
   Above that empty sleeve?

"Does a gold star in the window
   Now mean anything at all?

I wonder how my old girl feels
When she hears a bugle call.

"And that baby who sang
'Hello, Central, give me no man's land' —
Can they replace her daddy
With a military band?

"I wonder if the profiteers
Have satisfied their greed?
I wonder if a soldier's mother
Ever is in need?

"I wonder if the kings, who planned it all
Are really satisfied?
They played their game of checkers
And eleven million died.

"I am the Unknown Soldier
And maybe I died in vain,
But if I were alive and my country called,
I'd do it all over again."

Billy Rose

288

Here Dead Lie We

Here dead lie we because we did not choose
  To live and shame the land from which we
    sprung.
Life, to be sure, is nothing much to lose;
  But young men think it is, and we were
    young.

A. E. Housman

Faith and Inspiration

The Lord Is My Shepherd

The Lord is my shepherd; I shall not want.
He maketh me to lie down in green pastures:
   he leadeth me beside the still waters.
He restoreth my soul: he leadeth me in the
   paths of righteousness for his name's sake.
Yea, though I walk through the valley of the
   shadow of death, I will fear no evil: for thou
   art with me; thy rod and thy staff they
   comfort me.
Thou preparest a table before me in the
   presence of mine enemies: thou anointest my
   head with oil; my cup runneth over.
Surely goodness and mercy shall follow me all
   the days of my life: and I will dwell in the
   house of the Lord forever.

Psalm 23

Prayer of St. Francis of Assisi for Peace

Lord, make me an instrument of Your peace.
Where there is hatred, let me sow love;
Where there is injury, pardon;
Where there is doubt, faith;

Where there is despair, hope;
Where there is darkness, light;
And where there is sadness, joy.
O Divine Master, grant that I may not so much
    seek to be consoled as to console;
To be understood as to understand;
To be loved as to love;
For it is in giving that we receive;
It is in pardoning that we are pardoned;
And it is in dying that we are born to eternal
    life.

St. Francis of Assisi

Discipline

Throw away Thy rod,
Throw away Thy wrath;
    O my God,
Take the gentle path!

For my heart's desire
Unto Thine is bent:
    I aspire
To a full consent.

Not a word or look
I affect to own,
    But by book,
And Thy Book alone.

Though I fail, I weep;
Though I halt in pace,
  Yet I creep
To the throne of grace.

Then let wrath remove;
Love will do the deed;
  For with love
Stony hearts will bleed.

Love is swift of foot;
Love's a man of war,
  And can shoot,
And can hit from far.

Who can 'scape his bow?
That which wrought on Thee,
  Brought Thee low,
Needs must work on me.

Throw away Thy rod;
Though man frailties hath,
  Thou art God:
Throw away Thy wrath.
                    George Herbert

An Ode

The spacious firmament on high,
With all the blue ethereal sky,
And spangled heavens, a shining frame,
Their great Original proclaim.
The unwearied sun from day to day
Does his Creator's power display,
And publishes to every land
The work of an almighty Hand

Soon as the evening shades prevail,
The moon takes up the wondrous tale,
And nightly, to the listening earth,
Repeats the story of her birth;
Whilst all the stars that round her burn,
And all the planets in their turn,
Confirm the tidings as they roll,
And spread the truth from pole to pole.

What though in solemn silence all
Move round the dark terrestrial ball?
What though nor real voice nor sound
Amid their radiant orbs be found?
In reason's ear they all rejoice,
And utter forth a glorious voice,
Forever singing as they shine,
"The Hand that made us is divine!"

Joseph Addison

The Universal Prayer

Father of all! in every age,
   In every clime adored,
By saint, by savage, and by sage,
   Jehovah, Jove, or Lord!

Though great First Cause, least understood,
   Who all my sense confined
To know but this, that thou art good,
   And that myself am blind;

Yet gave me, in this dark estate,
   To see the good from ill;
And, binding nature fast in fate,
   Left free the human will:

What conscience dictates to be done,
   Or warns me not to do,
This, teach me more than hell to shun,
   That, more than heaven pursue.

What blessings thy free bounty gives
   Let me not cast away;
For God is paid when man receives,
   To enjoy is to obey.

Yet not to earth's contracted span
   Thy goodness let me bound,
Or think thee Lord alone of man,

When thousand worlds are round:

Let not this weak, unknowing hand
    Presume thy bolts to throw,
And deal damnation round the land
    On each I judge thy foe.

If I am right; thy grace impart
    Still in the right to stay;
If I am wrong, O, teach my heart
    To find that better way!

Save me alike from foolish pride
    And impious discontent
At aught thy wisdom has denied,
    Or aught thy goodness lent.

Teach me to feel another's woe,
    To hide the fault I see;
That mercy I to others show,
    That mercy show to me.

Mean though I am, not wholly so,
    Since quickened by thy breath;
O, lead me wheresoe'er I go,
    Through this day's life or death!

This day be bread and peace my lot;
    All else beneath the sun,
Thou know'st if best bestowed or not,

And let thy will be done.

To thee, whose temple is all space,
  Whose altar, earth, sea, skies,
One chorus let all Being raise,
  All Nature's incense rise!
                 Alexander Pope

Light Shining Out of Darkness

God moves in a mysterious way
  His wonders to perform;
He plants his footsteps in the sea,
  And rides upon the storm.

Deep in unfathomable mines,
  With never-failing skill
He treasures up his bright designs,
  And works his sovereign will.

Ye fearful saints, fresh courage take;
  The clouds ye so much dread
Are big with mercy, and shall break
  In blessings on your head.

Judge not the Lord by feeble sense,
  But trust him for his grace;
Behind a frowning providence
  He hides a smiling face.

His purposes will ripen fast,
  Unfolding every hour;
The bud may have a bitter taste,
  But sweet will be the flower.

Blind unbelief is sure to err,
  And scan his work in vain;
God is his own interpreter,
  And he will make it plain.

William Cowper

Verses

(Supposed to be written by Alexander Selkirk during his solitary abode on the island of Juan Fernandez)

I am monarch of all I survey;
My right there is none to dispute;
From the center all round to the sea
I am lord of the fowl and the brute.
O Solitude! where are the charms
That sages have seen in thy face?
Better dwell in the midst of alarms,
Than reign in this horrible place.

I am out of humanity's reach,
I must finish my journey alone,

Never hear the sweet music of speech;
I start at the sound of my own.
The beasts that roam over the plain
My form with indifference see;
They are so unacquainted with man,
Their tameness is shocking to me.

Society, Friendship, and Love,
Divinely bestowed upon man,
O, had I the wings of a dove
How soon would I taste you again!
My sorrows I then might assuage
In the ways of religion and truth,
Might learn from the wisdom of age,
And be cheered by the sallies of youth.

Religion! what treasure untold
Resides in that heavenly word!
More precious than silver and gold,
Or all that this earth can afford.
But the sound of the church-going bell
These valleys and rocks never heard,
Nor sighed at the sound of a knell,
Or smiled when a Sabbath appeared.
Ye winds, that have made me your sport,
Convey to this desolate shore
Some cordial endearing report
Of a land I shall visit no more:
My friends, — do they now and then send
A wish or a thought after me?

O tell me I yet have a friend,
Though a friend I am never to see.

How fleet is a glance of the mind!
Compared with the speed of its flight,
The tempest itself lags behind,
And the swift-winged arrows of light.
When I think of my own native land,
In a moment I seem to be there;
But alas! recollection at hand
Soon hurries me back to despair.

But the sea-fowl is gone to her nest,
The beast is laid down in his lair;
Even here is a season of rest,
And I to my cabin repair.
There's mercy in every place,
And mercy, encouraging thought!
Gives even affliction a grace
And reconciles man to his lot.

William Cowper

Death

I am a stranger in the land
   Where my forefathers trod;
A stranger I unto each heart,
   But not unto my God!

I pass along the crowded streets,
  Unrecognized my name;
This thought will come amid regrets —
  My God is still the same!

I seek with joy my childhood's home,
  But strangers claim the sod;
Not knowing where my kindred roam,
  Still present is my God!

They tell me that my friends all sleep
  Beneath the valley clod;
Oh, is not faith submissive sweet!
  I have no friend save God!

Unknown

O God, the Rock of Ages

O God, the Rock of Ages,
  Who evermore hast been,
What time the tempest rages,
  Our dwelling-place serene:
Before Thy first creations,
  O Lord, the same as now,
To endless generations,
  The Everlasting Thou!

Our years are like the shadows
  On sunny hills that lie,

Or grasses in the meadows
   That blossom but to die:
A sleep, a dream, a story,
   By strangers quickly told,
An unremaining glory
   Of things that soon are old.

O Thou who canst not slumber,
   Whose light grows never pale,
Teach us aright to number
   Our years before they fail!
On us Thy mercy lighten,
   On us thy goodness rest,
And let Thy Spirit brighten
   The hearts Thyself hast blessed!
           Edward H. Bickersteth

Up-Hill

Does the road wind up-hill all the way?
   Yes, to the very end.
Will the day's journey take the whole long
   day?
   From morn to night, my friend.

But is there for the night a resting-place?
   A roof for when the slow dark hours begin.
May not the darkness hide it from my face?
   You cannot miss that inn.

Shall I meet other wayfarers at night?
Those who have gone before.
Then must I knock, or call when just in sight?
They will not keep you standing at that door.

Shall I find comfort, travel-sore and weak?
Of labour you shall find the sum.
Will there be beds for me and all who seek?
Yea, beds for all who come.
                    Christina Georgina Rossetti

If I Can Stop One Heart from Breaking

If I can stop one Heart from breaking
I shall not live in vain
If I can ease one Life the Aching
Or cool one Pain

Or help one fainting Robin
Unto his Nest again
I shall not live in Vain.
                    Emily Dickinson

I Never Saw a Moor

I never saw a Moor —
I never saw the Sea —
Yet know I how the Heather looks

And what a Billow be.

I never spoke with God
Nor visited in Heaven —
Yet certain am I of the spot
As if the Checks were given —
Emily Dickinson

A Ballad of Trees and the Master

Into the woods my Master went,
Clean forspent, forspent.
Into the woods my Master came,
Forspent with love and shame.
But the olives they were not blind to Him;
The little gray leaves were kind to Him;
The thorn-tree had a mind to Him
When into the woods He came.

Out of the woods my Master went,
And He was well content.
Out of the woods my Master came,
Content with death and shame.
When Death and Shame would woo Him last,
From under the trees they drew Him last:
'Twas on a tree they slew Him — last
When out of the woods He came.
Sidney Lanier

A Life-Lesson

There! little girl, don't cry!
  They have broken your doll, I know;
    And your tea-set blue,
    And your play-house, too,
  Are things of the long ago;
    But childish troubles will soon pass by. —
    There! little girl, don't cry!

There! little girl, don't cry!
  They have broken your slate, I know;
    And the glad, wild ways
    Of your school-girl days
  Are things of the long ago;
    But life and love will soon come by. —
    There! little girl, don't cry!

There! little girl, don't cry!
  They have broken your heart, I know;
    And the rainbow gleams
    Of your youthful dreams
  Are things of the long ago;
    But Heaven holds all for which you
      sigh.—
    There! little girl, don't cry!

James Whitcomb Riley

The Winds of Fate

One ship drives east and another drives west
With the selfsame winds that blow.
   'Tis the set of the sails
   And not the gales
Which tells us the way to go.

Like the winds of the sea are the ways of fate,
   As we voyage along through life:
      'Tis the set of a soul
      That decides its goal,
   And not the calm or the strife.

Ella Wheeler Wilcox

Solitude

Laugh, and the world laughs with you;
   Weep, and you weep alone,
For the sad old earth must borrow its mirth,
   But has trouble enough of its own.
Sing, and the hills will answer;
   Sigh, it is lost on the air,
The echoes bound to a joyful sound,
   But shrink from voicing care.

Rejoice, and men will seek you;
   Grieve, and they turn and go.
They want full measure of all your pleasure,

But they do not need your woe.
Be glad, and your friends are many;
  Be sad, and you lose them all, —
There are none to decline your nectared wine,
  But alone you must drink life's gall.

Feast, and your halls are crowded;
  Fast, and the world goes by.
Succeed and give, and it helps you live,
  But no man can help you die.
There is room in the halls of pleasure
  For a long and lordly train,
But one by one we must all file on
  Through the narrow aisles of pain.
                    Ella Wheeler Wilcox

How Far to Bethlehem?

"How far is it to Bethlehem Town?"
Just over Jerusalem hills adown,
Past lovely Rachel's white-domed tomb —
Sweet shrine of motherhood's young doom.

"It isn't far to Bethlehem Town —
Just over the dusty roads adown,
Past Wise Men's well, still offering
Cool draughts from welcome wayside spring;
Past shepherds with their flutes of reed
That charm the woolly sheep they lead;

Past boys with kites on hilltop flying,
And soon you're there where Bethlehem's
  lying.
Sunned white and sweet on olived slopes,
Gold-lighted still with Judah's hopes.

"And so we find the Shepherd's field
And plain that gave rich Boaz yield,
And look where Herod's villa stood.
We thrill that earthly parenthood
Could foster Christ who was all-good;
And thrill that Bethlehem Town to-day
Looks down on Christmas homes that pray.

"It isn't far to Bethlehem Town!
It's anywhere that Christ comes down
And finds in people's friendly face
A welcome and abiding place.
The road to Bethlehem runs right through
The homes of folks like me and you."

                    Madeleine Sweeny Miller

Life's Lessons

I learn, as the years roll onward
   And leave the past behind,
Tht much I had counted sorrow
   But proves that God is kind;
That many a flower I had longed for
   Had hidden a thorn of pain,
And many a rugged bypath
   Led to fields of ripened grain.

The clouds that cover the sunshine
   They can not banish the sun;
And the earth shines out the brighter
   When the weary rain is done.
We must stand in the deepest shadow
   To see the clearest light;
And often through wrong's own darkness
   Comes the very strength of light.

The sweetest rest is at even,
   After a wearisome day,
When the heavy burden of labor
   Has borne from our hearts away;
And those who have never known sorrow
   Can not know the infinite peace
That falls on the troubled spirit
   When it sees at least release.

We must live through the dreary winter
If we would value the spring;
And the woods must be cold and silent
Before the robins sing.
The flowers must be buried in darkness
Before they can bud and bloom,
And the sweetest, warmest sunshine
Comes after the storm and gloom.

Unknown

A Prayer in Darkness

This much, O heaven — if I should brood or
    rave,
  Pity me not; but let the world be fed,
  Yea, in my madness if I strike me dead,
Heed you the grass that grows upon my grave.

If I dare snarl between this sun and sod,
  Whimper and clamor, give me grace to own,
  In sun and rain and fruit in season shown,
The shining silence of the scorn of God.

Thank God the stars are set beyond my power,
  If I must travail in a night of wrath;
  Thank God my tears will never vex a moth,
Nor any curse of mine cut down a flower.

Men say the sun was darkened: yet I had
  Thought it beat brightly, even on —
    Calvary:
  And He that hung upon the Torturing Tree
Heard all the crickets singing, and was glad.

                          G.K. Chesterton

The Donkey

When fishes flew and forests walked
   And figs grew upon thorn,
Some moment when the moon was blood
   Then surely I was born;

With monstrous head and sickening cry
   And ears like errant wings,
The devil's walking parody
   On all four-footed things;

The tattered outlaw of the earth,
   Of ancient crooked will:
Starve, scourge, deride me: I am dumb,
   I keep my secret still.

Fools! For I also had my hour;
   One far fierce hour and sweet;
There was shout about my ears,
   And palms before my feet.

G.K. Chesterton

Which Are You?

I watched them tearing a building down,
A gang of men in a busy town;
With a ho-heave-ho and a lusty yell
They swung a beam and the sidewalk fell.
I asked the foreman: "Are these men skilled,
And the men you'd hire if you had to build?"
He gave a laugh and said: "No indeed!
Just common labor is all I need.
I can easily wreck in a day or two
What builders have taken a year to do!"

And I thought to myself as I went my way,
Which of these roles have I tried to play?
Am I a builder who works with care,
Measuring life by the rule and square?
Am I shaping my deeds to a well-made plan,
Patiently doing the best I can?
Or am I a wrecker, who walks the town,
Content with the labor of tearing down.

Unknown

There Is No Death

There is a plan far greater than the plan you
   know;
There is a landscape broader than the one you
   see.
There is a haven where storm-tossed souls may
   go —
You call it death — we, immortality.

You call it death — this seeming endless sleep;
We call it birth — the soul at last set free.
'Tis hampered not by time or space — you
   weep.
Why weep at death? 'Tis immortality.

Farewell, dear voyageur — 'twill not be long.
Your work is done — now may peace rest with
   thee.
Your kindly thoughts and deeds — they will
   live on.
This is not death — 'tis immortality.

Farewell, dear voyageur — the river winds and
   turns;
The cadence of your song wafts near to me,
And now you know the thing that all men
   learn:
There is no death — there's immortality.

Unknown

O World

O world, thou choosest not the better part!
It is not wisdom to be only wise,
And on the inward vision close the eyes,
But it is wisdom to believe the heart.
Columbus found a world, and had no chart,
Save one that faith deciphered in the skies;
To trust the soul's invincible surmise
Was all his science and his only art.
Our knowledge is a torch of smoky pine
That lights the pathway but one step ahead
Across a void of mystery and dread.
Bid, then, the tender light of faith to shine
By which alone the mortal heart is led
Unto the thinking of the thought divine.

George Santayana

Reflection and Contemplation

On His Blindness

When I consider how my light is spent
Ere half my days in this dark world and wide,
And that one talent, which is death to hide,
Lodged with me useless, though my soul more
    bent
To serve therewith my Maker, and present
My true account, lest He returning chide;
"Doth God exact day-labor, light denied?"
I fondly ask. But Patience, to prevent
That murmur, soon replies, "God doth not
    need
Either man's work or his own gifts; who best
Bear his mild yoke, they serve him best; his
    state
Is kingly; thousands at his bidding speed,
And post o'er land and ocean without rest;
They also serve who only stand and wait."

John Milton

Ode to Duty

Stern Daughter of the Voice of God!
O Duty! if that name thou love,
Who art a light to guide, a rod
To check the erring, and reprove;
Thou, who art victory and law
When empty terrors overawe;
From vain temptations dost set free;
And calm'st the weary strife of frail humanity!

There are who ask not if thine eye
Be on them; who, in love and truth,
Where no misgiving is, rely
Upon the genial sense of youth:
Glad Hearts! without reproach or blot
Who do thy work, and know it not:
O if through confidence misplaced
They fail, thy saving arms, dread Power,
    around them cast.

Serene will be our days and bright,
And happy will our nature be,
When love is an unerring light,
And joy its own security.
And they a blissful course may hold
Even now, who, not unwisely bold,
Live in the spirit of this creed;
Yet seek thy firm support, according to their
    need.

I, loving freedom, and untried;
No sport of every random gust,
Yet being to myself a guide,
Too blindly have reposed my trust:
And oft, when in my heart was heard
Thy timely mandate, I deferred
The task, in smoother walks to stray;
But thee I now would serve more strictly, if
   I may.

Through no disturbance of my soul,
Or strong compunction in me wrought,
I supplicate for thy control;
But in the quietness of thought:
Me this unchartered freedom tires;
I feel the weight of chance-desires:
My hopes no more must change their name,
I long for a repose that ever is the same.

Stern Lawgiver! yet thou dost wear
The Godhead's most benignant grace;
Nor know we anything so fair
As is the smile upon thy face:
Flowers laugh before thee on their beds
And fragrance in thy footing treads;
Thou dost preserve the stars from wrong;
And the most ancient heavens, through Thee,
   are fresh and strong.

To humbler functions, awful Power!

I call thee: I myself commend
Unto thy guidance from this hour;
Oh, let my weakness have an end!
Give unto me, made lowly wise,
The spirit of self-sacrifice;
The confidence of reason give;
And in the light of truth thy Bondman let me
    live!

William Wordsworth

The World Is Too Much with Us

The world is too much with us; late and soon,
Getting and spending, we lay waste our
    powers:
Little we see in Nature that is ours;
We have given our hearts away, a sordid boon!
This sea that bares her bosom to the moon,
The winds that will be howling at all hours,
And are up-gathered now like sleeping flowers;
For this, for everything, we are out of tune;
It moves us not.— Great God! I'd rather be
A Pagan suckled in a creed outworn;
So might I, standing on this pleasant lea,
Have glimpses that would make me less
    forlorn;
Have sight of Proteus rising from the sea;
Or hear old Triton blow his wreathed horn.

William Wordsworth

Time

Unfathomable Sea! whose waves are years,
    Ocean of Time, whose waters of deep woe
Are brackish with the salt of human tears!
    Thou shoreless flood, which in thy ebb and
        flow
Claspest the limits of mortality,
And sick of prey, yet howling on for more,
Vomitest thy wrecks on its inhospitable shore;
    Treacherous in calm, and terrible in storm,
      Who shall put forth on thee,
      Unfathomable Sea?

               Percy Bysshe Shelley

Sonnet

To one who has been long in city pent,
    'Tis very sweet to look into the fair
    And open face of heaven, — to breathe a
        prayer
Full in the smile of the blue firmament.
Who is more happy, when, with heart content,
    Fatigued he sinks into some pleasant lair
    Of wavy grass, and reads a debonair
And gentle tale of love and languishment?
    Returning home at evening, with an ear
Catching the notes of Philomel,— an eye
    Watching the sailing cloudlet's bright career,

He mourns that day so soon has glided by:
  E'en like the passage of an angel's tear
That falls through the clear ether silently.

John Keats

Compensation

Why should I keep holiday
  When other men have none?
Why but because, when these are gay,
  I sit and mourn alone?

And why, when mirth unseals all tongues,
  Should mine alone be dumb?
Ah! late I spoke to silent throngs,
  And now their hour is come.

Ralph Waldo Emerson

Experience

The lords of life, the lords of life,—
I saw them pass
In their own guise,
Like and unlike,
Portly and grim,—
Use and surprise,
Surface and dream,
Succession swift, and spectral wrong,

Temperament without a tongue,
And the inventor of the game
Omnipresent without name; —
Some to see, some to be guessed,
They marched from east to west:
Little man, least of all,
Among the legs of his guardians tall,
Walked about with puzzled look.
Him by the hand dear Nature took,
Dearest Nature, strong and kind,
Whispered, "Darling, never mind!
Tomorrow they will wear another face,
The founder thou; these are thy race!"

Ralph Waldo Emerson

The Past

The debt is paid,
The verdict said,
The Furies laid,
The plague is stayed,
All fortunes made;
Turn the key and bolt the door,
Sweet is death forevermore.
Nor haughty hope, nor swart chagrin,
Nor murdering hate, can enter in.
All is now secure and fast;
Not the gods can shake the past;
Flies-to the adamantine door

Bolted down forevermore.
None can re-enter there —
No thief so politic,
No Satan with a royal trick
Steal in by window, chink, or hole,
To bind or unbind, add what lacked,
Insert a leaf, or forge a name,
New-face or finish what is packed,
Alter or mend eternal fact.

Ralph Waldo Emerson

The Day is Done

The day is done, and the darkness
   Falls from the wings of Night,
As a feather is wafted downward
   From an eagle in his flight.

I see the lights of the village
   Gleam through the rain and the mist:
And a feeling of sadness comes o'er me,
   That my soul cannot resist:

A feeling of sadness and longing,
   That is not akin to pain,
And resembles sorrow only
   As the mist resembles the rain.

Come, read to me some poem,

Some simple and heartfelt lay,
That shall soothe this restless feeling,
And banish the thoughts of day.

Not from the grand old masters,
Not from the bards sublime,
Whose distant footsteps echo
Through the corridors of Time.

For, like strains of martial music,
Their mighty thoughts suggest
Life's endless toil and endeavor;
And to-night I long for rest.

Read from some humbler poet,
Whose songs gush'd from his heart,
As showers from the clouds of summer,
Or tears from the eyelids start;

Who, through long days of labor,
And nights devoid of ease,
Still heard in his soul the music
Of wonderful melodies.

Such songs have power to quiet
The restless pulse of care,
And come like the benediction
That follows after prayer.

Then read from the treasured volume
  The poem of thy choice;
And lend to the rhyme of the poet
  The beauty of thy voice.

And the night shall be fill'd with music,
  And the cares that infest the day
Shall fold their tents like the Arabs,
  And as silently steal away.
                    Henry Wadsworth Longfellow

The Rainy Day

The day is cold, and dark, and dreary;
It rains, and the wind is never weary;
The vine still clings to the moldering wall,
But at every gust the dead leaves fall,
  And the day is dark and dreary.

My life is cold, and dark, and dreary;
It rains, and the wind is never weary;
My thoughts still cling to the moldering Past,
But the hopes of youth fall thick in the blast
  And the days are dark and dreary.

Be still, sad heart! and cease repining;
Behind the clouds is the sun still shining;
  Thy fate is the common fate of all,

Into each life some rain must fall,
   Some days must be dark and dreary.
         Henry Wadsworth Longfellow

A Psalm of Life

Tell me not, in mournful numbers,
   Life is but an empty dream!—
For the soul is dead that slumbers,
   And things are not what they seem.

Life is real! Life is earnest!
   And the grave is not its goal;
Dust thou art, to dust returnest,
   Was not spoken of the soul.

Not enjoyment, and not sorrow,
   Is our destined end or way;
But to act, that each to-morrow
   Find us farther than to-day.

Art is long, and Time is fleeting,
   And our hearts, though stout and brave,
Still, like muffled drums, are beating
   Funeral marches to the grave.

In the world's broad field of battle,
   In the bivouac of Life,

331

Be not like dumb, driven cattle!
  Be a hero in the strife!

Trust no Future, howe'er pleasant!
  Let the dead Past bury its dead!
Act,— act in the living Present!
  Heart within, and God o'erhead!

Lives of great men all remind us
  We can make our lives sublime,
And, departing, leave behind us
  Footprints on the sands of time;

Footprints, that perhaps another,
  Sailing o'er life's solemn main,
A forlorn and shipwrecked brother,
  Seeing, shall take heart again.

Let us, then, be up and doing,
  With a heart for any fate;
Still achieving, still pursuing,
  Learn to labor and to wait.
            Henry Wadsworth Longfellow

Last Lines

No coward soul is mine,
No trembler in the world's storm-troubled
  sphere:

I see Heaven's glories shine,
And faith shines equal, arming me from fear.

O God, within my breast,
Almighty, ever-present Deity!
    Life — that in me has rest,
As I — undying Life — have power in Thee!

Vain are the thousand creeds
That move men's hearts: unutterably vain;
    Worthless as withered weeds,
Or idlest froth amid the boundless main.

To waken doubt in one
Holding so fast by thine infinity;
    So surely anchored on
The steadfast rock of immortality.

With wide-embracing love
Thy Spirit animates eternal years,
    Pervades and broods above,
Changes, sustains, dissolves, creates, and
        rears.

Though earth and man were gone,
And suns and universes ceased to be,
    And Thou were left alone,
Every existence would exist in Thee.

There is not room for Death,
Nor atom that his might could render void:
Thou — Thou art Being and Breath,
And what Thou art may never be destroyed.

Emily Brontë

The Old Stoic

Riches I hold in light esteem,
  And Love I laugh to scorn;
And lust of fame was but a dream
  That vanished with the morn:

And if I pray, the only prayer
  That moves my lips for me
Is, "Leave the heart that now I bear,
  And give me liberty!"

Yes, as my swift days near their goal,
  'Tis all that I implore;
Through life and death a chainless soul,
  With courage to endure.

Emily Brontë

Success Is Counted Sweetest

Success is counted sweetest
By those who ne'er succeed.
To comprehend a nectar
Requires sorest need.

Not one of all the purple Host
Who took the Flag today
Can tell the definition
So clear of Victory

As he defeated — dying —
On whose forbidden ear,
The distant strains of triumph
Burst agonized and clear!
Emily Dickinson

Invictus

Out of the night that covers me,
  Black as the Pit from pole to pole,
I thank whatever gods may be
  For my unconquerable soul.

In the fell clutch of circumstance
  I have not winced nor cried aloud.
Under the bludgeonings of chance
  My head is bloody, but unbowed.

Beyond this place of wrath and tears
　Looms but the Horror of the shade,
And yet the menance of the years
　Finds and shall find me unafraid.

It matters not how strait the gate,
　How charged with punishments the scroll,
I am the master of my fate:
　I am the captain of my soul.

William Ernest Henley

The Right Kind of People

Gone is the city, gone is the day,
Yet still the story and the meaning stay:
Once where a prophet in the palm shade
　basked
A traveler chanced at noon to rest his miles.
"What sort of people may they be," he asked,
"In this proud city on the plains o'erspread?"
"Well, friend, what sort of people whence you
　came?"
"What sort?" the packman scowled; "why,
　knaves and fools."
"You'll find the people here the same," the
　wise man said.

Another stranger in the dusk drew near,
And pausing, cried "What sort of people here

In your bright city where yon towers arise?"
"Well, friend, what sort of people whence you
    came?"
"What sort?" the pilgrim smiled,
"Good, true and wise."
"You'll find the people here the same,"
The wise man said.
Edwin Markham

Outwitted

He drew a circle that shut me out —
Heretic, rebel, a thing to flout.
But Love and I had the wit to win:
We drew a circle that took him in!
Edwin Markham

If

If you can keep your head when all about you
    Are losing theirs and blaming it on you;
If you can trust yourself when all men doubt
        you,
    But make allowance for their doubting too;
If you can wait and not be tired by waiting,
    Or, being lied about, don't deal in lies,
Or, being hated, don't give way to hating,

And yet don't look too good, nor talk too
wise;

If you can dream — and not make dreams your
master;
If you can think — and not make thoughts
your aim;
If you can meet with triumph and disaster
And treat those two imposters just the same;
If you can bear to hear the truth you've spoken
Twisted by knaves to make a trap for fools,
Or watch the things you gave your life
to broken,
And stoop and build'em up with wornout
tools;

If you can make one heap of all your winnings
And risk it on one turn of pitch-and-toss,
And lose, and start again at your beginnings
And never breathe a word about your loss;
If you can force your heart and nerve and
sinew
To serve your turn long after they are gone,
And so hold on when there is nothing in you
Except the Will which says to them: "Hold
on";

If you can talk with crowds and keep your
virtue,
Or walk with kings — nor lose the common

touch;
If neither foes nor loving friends can hurt you;
   If all men count with you, but none too
      much;
If you can fill the unforgiving minute
   With sixty seconds' worth of distance run —
Yours is the Earth and everything that's in it,
   And — which is more — you'll be a Man,
      my son!

Rudyard Kipling

The Winners

What is the moral? Who rides may read.
When the night is thick and the tracks are
   blind,
A friend at a pinch is a friend indeed,
But a fool to wait for the laggard behind.
Down to Gehenna or up to the Throne,
He travels the fastest who travels alone.

White hands cling to the tightened rein,
Slipping the spur from the booted heel,
Tenderest voices cry "Turn again,"
Red lips tarnish the scabbarded steel,
High hopes faint on a warm hearth stone —
He travels the fastest who travels alone.

One may fall but he falls by himself —

Falls by himself with himself to blame,
One may attain and to him is the pelf,
Loot of the city in Gold or Fame.
Plunder of earth shall be all his own
Who travels the fastest and travels alone.

Wherefore the more be ye holpen and
    stayed —
Stayed by a friend in the hour of toil,
Sing the heretical song I have made —
His be the labor and yours be the spoil.
Win by his aid and the aid disown —
He travels the fastest who travels alone!

Rudyard Kipling

Progress

Let there be many windows to your soul,
That all the glory of the universe
May beautify it. Not the narrow pane
Of one poor creed can catch the radiant rays
That shine from countless sources. Tear away
The blinds of superstition; let the light
Pour through fair windows broad as Truth itself
And high as God.
                    Why should the spirit peer
Through some priest-curtained orifice, and
    grope
Along dim corridors of doubt, when all

The splendor from unfathomed seas of space
Might bathe it with the golden waves of Love?
Sweep up the débris of decaying faiths;
Sweep down the cobwebs of worn-out beliefs,
And throw your soul wide open to the light
Of Reason and of Knowledge. Tune your ear
To all the wordless music of the stars
And to the voice of Nature, and your heart
Shall turn to truth and goodness as the plant
Turns to the sun. A thousand unseen hands
Reach down to help you to their peace-
　　crowned heights,
And all the forces of the firmament
Shall fortify your strength. Be not afraid
To thrust aside half-truths and grasp the whole.
Ella Wheeler Wilcox

Will

There is no chance, no destiny, no fate,
　　Can circumvent or hinder or control
　　The firm resolve of a determined soul.
Gifts count for nothing; will alone is great;
All things give way before it, soon or late.
　　What obstacle can stay the mighty force
　　Of the sea-seeking river in its course,
Or cause the ascending orb of day to wait?

Each wellborn soul must win what it deserves.
Let the fool prate of luck. The fortunate
　　Is he whose earnest purpose never
　　　　swerves,
　　Whose slightest action or inaction serves
The one great aim. Why, even Death stands
　　still,
And waits an hour sometimes for such a will.
Ella Wheeler Wilcox

Worth While

It is easy enough to be pleasant,
　　When life flows by like a song,
But the man worth while is one who will
　　　　smile,
　　When everything goes dead wrong.
For the test of the heart is trouble,
　　And it always comes with the years,
And the smile that is worth the praises of earth
　　Is the smile that shines through tears.

It is easy enough to be prudent,
　　When nothing tempts you to stray,
When without or within no voice of sin
　　Is luring your soul away;
But it's only a negative virtue
　　Until it is tried by fire,
And the life that is worth the honor on earth

Is the one that resists desire.

By the cynic, the sad, the fallen,
    Who had no strength for the strife,
The world's highway is cumbered to-day;
    They make up the sum of life.
But the virtue that conquers passion,
    And the sorrow that hides in a smile,
It is these that are worth the homage on earth
    For we find them but once in a while.

                        Ella Wheeler Wilcox

Growing Old

The days grow shorter, the nights grow longer;
    The headstones thicken along the way;
And life grows sadder, but love grows stronger
    For those who walk with us day by day.

The tear comes quicker, the laugh comes
        slower;
    The courage is lesser to do and dare;
And the tide of joy in the heart falls lower,
    And seldom covers the reefs of care.

But all true things in the world seem truer,
    And the better things of earth seem best,
And friends are dearer, as friends are fewer,
    And love is all as our sun dips west.

Then let us clasp hands as we walk together,
    And let us speak softly in low, sweet tone,
For no man knows on the morrow whether
    We two pass on — or but one alone.

Ella Wheeler Wilcox

Hold Fast Your Dreams

Hold fast your dreams!
Within your heart
Keep one still, secret spot
Where dreams may go,
And, sheltered so,
May thrive and grow
Where doubt and fear are not.
O keep a place apart,
Within your heart,
For little dreams to go!

Think still of lovely things that are not true.
Let wish and magic work at will in you.
Be sometimes blind to sorrow. Make believe!
Forget the calm that lies
In disillusioned eyes.
Though we all know that we must die,
Yet you and I
May walk like gods and be
Even now at home in immortality.

We see so many ugly things —
Deceits and wrongs and quarrelings;
We know, alas! we know
How quickly fade
The color in the west,
The bloom upon the flower,
The bloom upon the breast
And youth's blind hour.
Yet keep within your heart
A place apart
Where little dreams may go,
May thrive and grow.
Hold fast — hold fast your dreams!

Louise Driscoll

I Shall Not Pass This Way Again

Through this toilsome world, alas!
Once and only once I pass,
If a kindness I may show,
If a good deed I may do
To a suffering fellow man,
Let me do it while I can.
No delay, for it is plain
I shall not pass this way again.

Unknown

It Couldn't Be Done

Somebody said that it couldn't be done,
    But he with a chuckle replied
That "maybe it couldn't," but he would be
      one
    Who wouldn't say so till he'd tried.
So he buckled right in with the trace of a grin
    On his face. If he worried he hid it.
He started to sing as he tackled the thing
    That couldn't be done, and he did it.

Somebody scoffed: "Oh, you'll never do that;
    At least no one ever has done it";
But he took off his coat and he took off his
      hat,
    And the first thing we knew he'd begun it.
With a lift of his chin and a bit of a grin,
    Without any doubting or quiddit,
He started to sing as he tackled the thing
    That couldn't be done, and he did it.

There are thousands to tell you it cannot be
      done,
    There are thousands to prophesy failure;
There are thousands to point out to you, one
      by one,
    The dangers that wait to assail you.
But just buckle in with a bit of a grin,
    Just take off your coat and go to it;

Just start to sing as you tackle the thing
That "cannot be done," and you'll do it.
Edgar A. Guest

The Lord God Planted a Garden

The Lord God planted a garden
In the first white days of the world,
And he set there an angel warden
In a garment of light enfurled.

So near to the peace of Heaven,
That the hawk might nest with the wren,
For there in the cool of the even'
God walked with the first of men.

The kiss of the sun for pardon,
The song of the birds for mirth —
One is nearer God's heart in a garden
Than anywhere else on earth.
Dorothy Frances Gurney

Don't Quit

When things go wrong, as they sometimes
will,
When the road you're trudging seems all up
hill,

When the funds are low and the debts are high,
And you want to smile, but you have to sigh,
When care is pressing you down a bit,
Rest, if you must — but don't you quit.

Life is queer with its twists and turns,
As everyone of us sometimes learns,
And many a failure turns about
When he might have won had he stuck it out;
Don't give up, though the pace seems slow —
You might succeed with another blow.

Often the goal is nearer than
It seems to a faint and faltering man,
Often the struggler has given up
When he might have captured the victor's cup.
And he learned too late, when the night slipped
    down,
How close he was to the golden crown.

Success is failure turned inside out —
The silver tint of the clouds of doubt —
And you never can tell how close you are,
It may be near when it seems afar;
So stick to the fight when you're hardest hit —
It's when things seem worst that you mustn't
    quit.

Unknown

Emancipation

I work or play, as I think best;
   I fare abroad, or stay at home;
When weary, I sit down and rest;
   I bid one go, another come —
     Because I'm sixty!

When whistles blow with clamorous hue,
   I rouse me not, as I was wont.
I do the things I like to do,
   And leave undone the things I don't —
     Because I'm sixty!

I grow not blind, nor deaf, nor lame,
   I still can dance, and hear, and see,
But love the restful book or game;
   No more the strenuous life for me,
     I quit at sixty!

My toilet is my fondest care,
   The serial story I peruse;
I glory in my silvering hair,
   I love my comfortable shoes —
     I'm glad I'm sixty!

Let youngsters lift the weary load,
   And the burden tug and strain:
I love the easy, downward road;

I would not climb life's hill again —
Glory be! I'm sixty!

Unknown

When You Are Old

When you are old and grey and full of sleep,
And nodding by the fire, take down this book
And slowly read, and dream of the soft look
Your eyes had once, and of their shadows
    deep;

How many loved your moments of glad grace,
And loved your beauty with love false or true;
But one man loved the pilgrim soul in you,
And loved the sorrows of your changing face.

And bending down beside the glowing bars
Murmur, a little sadly, how love fled
And paced upon the mountains overhead
And hid his face amid a crowd of stars.

William Butler Yeats

On Growing Old

Be with me, Beauty, for the fire is dying;
My dog and I are old, too old for roving.
Man, whose young passion sets the spindrift
    flying,
Is soon too lame to march, too cold for loving.
I take the book and gather to the fire,
Turning old yellow leaves; minute by minute
The clock ticks to my heart. A withered wire
Moves a thin ghost of music in the spinet.
I cannot sail your seas, I cannot wander
Your cornland, nor your hill-land nor your
    valleys
Ever again, nor share the battle yonder
Where the young knight the broken squadron
    rallies.
Only stay quiet while my mind remembers
The beauty of fire from the beauty of embers.

Beauty, have pity! for the strong have power,
The rich their wealth, the beautiful their grace,
Summer of man its sunlight and its flower,
Spring-time of man all April in a face.
Only, as in the jostling in the Strand,
Where the mob thrusts or loiters or is loud
The beggar with the saucer in his hand
Asks only a penny from the passing crowd,
So, from this glittering world with all its
    fashion,

Its fire, and play of men, its stir, its march,
Let me have wisdom, Beauty, wisdom and
    passion,
Bread to the soul, rain where the summers
    parch.
Give me but these, and, though the darkness
    close
Even the night will blossom as the rose.

John Masefield

The Road Not Taken

Two roads diverged in a yellow wood,
And sorry I could not travel both
And be one traveler, long I stood
And looked down one as far as I could
To where it bent in the undergrowth;

Then took the other, as just as fair,
And having perhaps the better claim,
Because it was grassy and wanted wear;
Though as for that the passing there
Had worn them really about the same,

And both that morning equally lay
In leaves no step had trodden black.
Oh, I kept the first for another day!
Yet knowing how way leads on to way,
I doubted if I should ever come back.

I shall be telling this with a sigh
Somewhere ages and ages hence:
Two roads diverged in a wood, and I —
I took the one less traveled by,
And that has made all the difference.

Robert Frost

Humor

Elegy on the Death of a Mad Dog

Good people all, of every sort,
  Give ear unto my song;
And if you find it wond'rous short,
  It cannot hold you long.

In Islington there was a man,
  Of whom the world might say,
That still a godly race he ran,
  Whene'er he went to pray.

A kind and gentle heart he had,
  To comfort friends and foes;
The naked every day he clad,
  When he put on his clothes.

And in that town a dog was found,
  As many dogs there be,
Both mongrel, puppy, whelp, and hound,
  And curs of low degree.

This dog and man at first were friends;
  But when a pique began,
The dog, to gain some private ends,
  Went mad and bit the man.

357

Around from all the neighboring streets
   The wond'ring neighbors ran,
And swore the dog had lost its wits,
   To bit so good a man.

The wound it seem'd both sore and sad
   To every Christian eye;
And while they swore the dog was mad,
   They swore the man would die.

But soon a wonder came to light,
   That showed the rogues they lied:
The man recover'd of the bite,
   The dog it was that died.

Oliver Goldsmith

Sorrows of Werther

Werther had a love for Charlotte
   Such as words could never utter;
Would you know how first he met her?
   She was cutting bread and butter.

Charlotte was a married lady,
   And a moral man was Werther,
And for all the wealth of Indies
   Would do nothing for to hurt her.

So he sighed and pined and ogled,

And his passion boiled and bubbled,
Till he blew his silly brains out,
    And no more was by it troubled.

Charlotte, having seen his body
    Borne before her on a shutter,
Like a well-conducted person,
    Went on cutting bread and butter.
                    William Makepeace Thackeray

The Height of the Ridiculous

I wrote some lines once on a time
    In wondrous merry mood,
And thought, as usual, men would say
    They were exceeding good.

They were so queer, so very queer,
    I laughed as I would die;
Albeit, in the general way,
    A sober man am I.

I called my servant, and he came;
    How kind it was of him
To mind a slender man like me,
    He of the mighty limb!

"These to the printer," I exclaimed,
    And, in my humorous way,

I added (as a trifling jest),
  "There'll be the devil to pay."

He took the paper, and I watched,
  And saw him peep within;
At the first line he read, his face
  Was all upon the grin.

He read the next; the grin grew broad,
  And shot from ear to ear;
He read the third; a chuckling noise
  I now began to hear.

The fourth; he broke into a roar;
  The fifth; his waistband split;
The sixth; he burst five buttons off,
  And tumbled in a fit.

Ten days and nights, with sleepless eye,
  I watched that wretched man,
And since, I never dare to write
  As funny as I can.

Oliver Wendell Holmes

The Owl and the Pussy-cat

The Owl and the Pussy-cat went to sea
  In a beautiful pea-green boat:
They took some honey, and plenty of money

360

Wrapped up in a five-pound note.
The Owl looked up to the stars above,
 And sang to a small guitar,
"O lovely Pussy, O Pussy, my love,
 What a beautiful Pussy you are,
  You are,
  You are!
 What a beautiful Pussy you are!"

Pussy said to the Owl, "You elegant fowl,
 How charmingly sweet you sing!
Oh! let us be married; too long we have
  tarried:
 But what shall we do for a ring?"
They sailed away, for a year and a day,
 To the land where the bong-tree grows;
And there in a wood a Piggy-wig stood,
 With a ring at the end of his nose.
  His nose,
  His nose,
 With a ring at the end of his nose

"Dear Pig, are you willing to sell for one
  shilling
 Your ring?" Said the Piggy, "I will."
So they took it away, and were married next
  day
 By the turkey who lives on the hill.
They dined on mince and slices of quince,
 Which they ate with a runcible spoon;

And hand in hand, on the edge of the sand,
They danced by the light of the moon,
The moon,
The moon,
They danced by the light of the moon.

Edward Lear

Incidents in the Life of My Uncle Arly

O my aged Uncle Arly!
Sitting on a heap of Barley
Thro' the silent hours of night, —
Close beside a leafy thicket: —
On his nose there was a Cricket, —
In his hat a Railway Ticket
(But his shoes were far too tight).

Long ago, in youth, he squander'd
All his goods away, and wander'd
To the Tiniskoop hills afar.
There on golden sunsets blazing,
Every evening found him gazing, —
Singing, — "Orb! you're quite amazing!
How I wonder what you are!"

Like the ancient Medes and Persians,
Always by his own exertions
He subsisted on those hills; —
Whiles, — by teaching children spelling, —

Or at times by merely yelling, —
Or at intervals by selling
"Propter's Nicodemus Pills."

Later, in his morning rambles
He perceived the moving brambles —
Something square and white disclose; —
'Twas a First-class Railway Ticket;
But, on stooping down to pick it
Off the ground, — a pea-green Cricket
Settled on my uncle's Nose.

Never — Never more, — oh! never,
Did that Cricket leave him ever, —
Dawn or evening, day or night; —
Clinging as a constant treasure, —
Chirping with a cheerious measure, —
Wholly to my uncle's pleasure
(Though his shoes were far too tight).

So for three and forty winters,
Till his shoes were worn to splinters,
All those hills he wandered o'er, —
Sometimes silent; — sometimes yelling; —
Till he came to Borley-Melling,
Near his old ancestral dwelling
(But his shoes were far too tight).

On a little heap of Barley
Died my aged Uncle Arly,

And they buried him one night; —
Close beside the leafy thicket; —
There, — his hat and Railway Ticket; —
There, — his ever-faithful Cricket
(But his shoes were far too tight).

Edward Lear

Jabberwocky

'Twas brillig and the slithy toves
  Did gyre and gimble in the wabe:
All mimsy were the borogoves,
  And the mome raths outgrabe.

"Beware the Jabberwock, my son!
  The jaws that bite, the claws that catch!
Beware the Jubjub bird, and shun
  The frumious Bandersnatch!"

He took his vorpal sword in hand;
  Long time the manxome foe he sought —
So rested he by the Tumtum tree,
  And stood awhile in thought.

And, as in uffish thought he stood,
  The Jabberwock, with eyes of flame,
Came whiffling through the tulgey wood,
  And burbled as it came!

One, two! One, two! And through and through
   The vorpal blade went snicker-snack!
He left it dead, and with its head
   He went galumphing back.

"And hast thou slain the Jabberwock?
   Come to my arms, my beamish boy!
O frabjous day! Callooh, Callay!"
   He chortled in his joy.

'Twas brillig, and the slithy toves
   Did gyre and gimble in the wabe:
All mimsy were the borogoves,
   And the mome raths outgrabe.

Lewis Carroll

The Walrus and the Carpenter

The sun was shining on the sea
   Shining with all his might:
He did his very best to make
   The billows smooth and bright —
And this was odd, because it was
   The middle of the night.

The moon was shining sulkily,
   Because she thought the sun
Had got no business to be there
   After the day was done —

"It's very rude of him," she said,
    "To come and spoil the fun!"

The sea was wet as wet could be,
    The sands were dry as dry.
You could not see a cloud, because
    No cloud was in the sky:
No birds were flying overhead —
    There were no birds to fly.

The Walrus and the Carpenter
    Were walking close at hand:
They wept like anything to see
    Such quantities of sand.
"If this were only cleared away,"
    They said, "it *would* be grand!"

"If seven maids with seven mops
    Swept it for half a year,
Do you suppose," the Walrus said,
    "That they could get it clear?"
"I doubt it," said the Carpenter,
    And shed a bitter tear.

"O Oysters, come and walk with us!"
    The Walrus did beseech.
"A pleasant talk, a pleasant walk,
    Along the briny beach:
We cannot do with more than four,
    To give a hand to each."

The eldest Oyster looked at him,
　　But never a word he said:
The eldest Oyster winked his eye,
　　And shook his heavy head —
Meaning to say he did not choose
　　To leave the oyster-bed.

But four young Oysters hurried up,
　　All eager for the treat:
Their coats were brushed, their faces washed,
　　Their shoes were clean and neat —
And this was odd, because, you know,
　　They hadn't any feet.

Four other Oysters followed them,
　　And yet another four;
And thick and fast they came at last,
　　And more, and more, and more —
All hopping through the frothy waves,
　　And scrambling to the shore.

The Walrus and the Carpenter
　　Walked on a mile or so,
And then they rested on a rock
　　Conveniently low:
And all the little Oysters stood
　　And waited in a row.

"The time has come," the Walrus said,
　　"To talk of many things:

Of shoes and ships and sealing-wax,
  Of cabbages and kings;
And why the sea is boiling hot —
  And whether pigs have wings."

"But wait a bit," the Oysters cried,
  "Before we have our chat;
For some of us are out of breath,
  And all of us are fat!"

"No hurry!" said the Carpenter.
  They thanked him much for that.

"A loaf of bread," the Walrus said,
  "Is what we chiefly need:
Pepper and vinegar besides
  Are very good indeed —
Now, if you're ready, Oysters dear,
  We can begin to feed."

"But not on us!" the Oysters cried,
  Turning a little blue.
"After such kindness, that would be
  A dismal thing to do!"
"The night is fine," the Walrus said.
  "Do you admire the view?"

"It was so kind of you to come!
  And you are very nice!"
The Carpenter said nothing but

"Cut us another slice.
I wish you were not quite so deaf —
    I've had to ask you twice!"

"It seems a shame," the Walrus said,
    "To play them such a trick,
After we've brought them out so far,
    And made them trot so quick!"
The Carpenter said nothing but
    "The butter's spread too thick!"

"I weep for you," the Walrus said:
    "I deeply sympathize."
With sobs and tears he sorted out
    Those of the largest size,
Holding his pocket-handkerchief
    Before his streaming eyes.

"O Oysters," said the Carpenter,
    "You've had a pleasant run!
Shall we be trotting home again?"
    But answer came there none —
And this was scarely odd, because
    They'd eaten every one.

Lewis Carroll

Father William

(After Southey)

"You are old, Father William," the young
    man said.
  "And your hair has become very white;
And yet you incessantly stand on your head —
  Do you think, at your age, it is right?"

"In my youth," Father William replied to his
    son,
  "I feared it might injure the brain;
But, now that I'm perfectly sure I have none,
  Why, I do it again and again."

"You are old," said the youth, "as I
    mentioned before,
  And have grown most uncommonly fat;
Yet you turned a back-somersault in at the
    door —
  Pray, what is the reason of that?"

"In my youth," said the sage, as he shook his
    gray locks,
  "I kept all my limbs very supple
By the use of this ointment — one shilling the
    box —
  Allow me to sell you a couple?"

"You are old," said the youth, "and your
 jaws are too weak
For anything tougher than suet;
Yet you finished the goose, with the bones and
 the beak —
Pray, how did you manage to do it?"

"In my youth," said his father, "I took to the
 law,
And argued each case with my wife;
And the muscular strength which it gave to my
 jaw,
Has lasted the rest of my life."

"You are old," said the youth, "one would
 hardly suppose
That your eye was as steady as ever;
Yet you balanced an eel on the end of your
 nose —
What made you so awfully clever?"

"I have answered three questions and that is
 enough,"
Said his father; "don't give yourself airs!
Do you think I can listen all day to such stuff?
Be off, or I'll kick you downstairs!"

Lewis Carroll

The Duel

The gingham dog and the calico cat
Side by side on the table sat;
'Twas half past twelve, and (what do you
    think!)
Nor one nor t'other had slept a wink!
    The old Dutch clock and the Chinese plate
    Appeared to know as sure as fate
There was going to be a terrible spat.
    (I wasn't there: I simply state
    What was told to me by the Chinese plate!)

The gingham dog went, "Bow-wow-wow!"
And the calico cat replied, "Mee-ow!"
The air was littered, an hour or so,
With bits of gingham and calico,
    While the old Dutch clock in the chimney-
    place
Up with its hands before its face,
For it always dreaded a family row!
    (Now mind; I'm only telling you
    What the old Dutch clock declares is true!)

The Chinese plate looked very blue,
And wailed, "Oh dear! what shall we do!"
But the gingham dog and the calico cat
Wallowed this way and tumbled that,
    Employing every tooth and claw
    In the awfullest way you ever saw —

And, oh! how the gingham and calico flew!
  (Don't fancy I exaggerate —
  I got my news from the Chinese plate!)

Next morning, where the two had sat
They found no trace of dog or cat:
And some folks think unto this day
That burglars stole that pair away!
  But the truth about the cat and pup
  Is this: they ate each other up!
Now what do you really think of that!
  (The old Dutch clock it told me so,
  And that is how I came to know.)
                                    Eugene Field

Jest 'Fore Christmas

Father calls me William, sister calls me Will,
Mother calls me Willie, but the fellers call me
    Bill!
Mighty glad I ain't a girl — ruther be a boy,
Without them sashes, curls, an' things that's
    worn by Fauntleroy!
Love to chawnk green apples an' go swimmin'
    in the lake —
Hate to take the castor-ile they give for belly-
    ache!
'Most all the time, the whole year round, there
    ain't no flies on me,

But jest 'fore Christmas I'm as good as I kin be!

Got a yeller dog named Sport, sick him on the cat;
First thing she knows she doesn't know where she is at!
Got a clipper sled, an' when us kids goes out to slide,
'Long comes the grocery cart, an' we all hook a ride!
But sometimes when the grocery man is worrited an' cross,
He reaches at us with his whip, an' larrups up his hoss,
An' then I laff an' holler, "Oh, ye never teched *me!*"
But jest 'fore Christmas I'm as good as I kin be!

Gran'ma says she hopes that when I git to be a man,
I'll be a missionarer like her oldest brother, Dan,
As was et up by the cannibuls that lives in Ceylon's Isle,
Where every prospeck pleases, an' only man is vile!
But gran'ma she has never been to see a Wild West show,

Nor read the Life of Daniel Boone, or else I
   guess she'd know
That Buff'lo Bill and cow-boys is good enough
   for me!
Excep' jest 'fore Christmas, when I'm good as
   I kin be!

And then old Sport he hangs around, so
   solemn-like an' still,
His eyes they keep a-sayin': "What's the
   matter, little Bill?"
The old cat sneaks down off her perch an'
   wonders what's become
Of them two enemies of hern that used to
   make things hum!
But I am so perlite an' 'tend so earnestly to
   biz,
That mother says to father: "How improved
   our Willie is!"
But father, havin' been a boy hisself,
   suspicions me
When jest 'fore Christmas, I'm as good as I
   kin be!

For Christmas, with its lots an' lots of candies,
   cakes an' toys,
Was made, they say, for proper kids an' not
   for naughty boys;
So wash yer face an' bresh yer hair, an' mind
   yer p's an' q's,

An' don't bust out yer pantaloons, an' don't
    wear out yer shoes;
Say "Yessum" to the ladies, an' "Yessur" to
    the men,
An' when they's company, don't pass yer plate
    for pie again;
But thinking of the things yer'd like to see
    upon that tree,
Jest 'fore Christmas be as good as yer kin be!
Eugene Field

Wishes Of An Elderly Man

(Wished at a Garden Party, June, 1914)

I wish I loved the Human Race;
I wish I loved its silly face;
I wish I liked the way it walks;
I wish I liked the way it talks;
And when I'm introduced to one
I wish I thought *What Jolly Fun!*
Walter Raleigh

Sestina of the Tramp-Royal

Speakin' in general, I 'ave tried 'em all —
The 'appy roads that take you o'er the world.
Speakin' in general, I 'ave found them good

For such as cannot use one bed too long,
But must get 'ence, the same as I 'ave done,
An' go observin' matters till they die.

What do it matter where or 'ow we die,
So long as we've our 'ealth to watch it all —
The different ways that different things are
    done,
An' men an' women lovin' in this world;
Takin' our chances as they come along,
An' when they ain't, pretendin' they are good?

In cash or credit — no, it aren't no good;
You 'ave to 'ave the 'abit or you'd die,
Unless you lived your life but one day long,
Nor didn't prophesy nor fret at all,
But drew your tucker some'ow from the world,
An' never bothered what you might ha' done.

But, Gawd, what things are they I 'aven't
    done!
I've turned my 'and to most, an' turned it
    good,
In various situations round the world —
For 'im that doth not work must surely die;
But that's no reason man should labor all
'Is life on one same shift — life's none so
    long.

Therefore, from job to job I've moved along.
Pay couldn't 'old me when my time was done,
For something in my 'ead upset it all,
Till I 'ad dropped whatever 't was for good,
An' out at sea, be'eld the dock-lights die,
An' met my mate — the wind that tramps the
    world!

It's like a book, I think, this bloomin' world,
Which you can read and care for just so long,
But presently you feel that you will die
Unless you get the page you're readin' done,
An' turn another — likely not so good;
But what you're after is to turn 'em all.

Gawd bless this world! Whatever she 'ath
done —
Excep' when awful long — I've found it good.
So write, before I die, " 'E liked it all!"
                              Rudyard Kipling

The Purple Cow
(Reflections on a Mythic Beast,
Who's Quite Remarkable, at Least.)

I never saw a Purple Cow;
   I never Hope to See One;
But I can Tell you, Anyhow,
   I'd rather See than Be One.
            Gelett Burgess

A Word of Encouragement

O what a tangled web we weave
When first we practice to deceive!
But when we've practiced quite a while
How vastly we improve our style!
               J. R. Pope

The Blind Men and the Elephant

It was six men of Indostan
   To learning much inclined,
Who went to see the elephant
   (Though all of them were blind),
That each by observation
   Might satisfy his mind.

The First approached the elephant,

And, happening to fall
Against his broad and sturdy side,
    At once began to bawl:
"God bless me! but the elephant
    Is nothing but a wall!"

The Second, feeling of the tusk,
    Cried: "Ho! what have we here
So very round and smooth and sharp?
    To me 'tis mighty clear
This wonder of an elephant
    Is very like a spear!"

The Third approached the animal,
    And, happening to take
The squirming trunk within his hands,
    Thus boldly up and spake:
"I see," quoth he, "the elephant
    Is very like a snake!"

The Fourth reached out his eager hand,
    And felt about the knee:
"What most this wondrous beast is like
    Is mighty plain," quoth he.
" 'Tis clear enough the elephant
    Is very like a tree."

The Fifth, who chanced to touch the ear,
    Said: "E'en the blindest man
Can tell what this resembles most;
    Deny the fact who can,

This marvel of an elephant
  Is very like a fan!"

The Sixth no sooner had begun
  About the beast to grope,
Than, seizing on the swinging tail
  That fell within his scope,
"I see," quoth he, "the elephant
  Is very like a rope!"

And so these men of Indostan
  Disputed loud and long,
Each in his own opinion
  Exceeding stiff and strong
Though each was partly in the right,
  And all were in the wrong!

So, oft in theologic wars
  The disputants, I ween,
Rail on in utter ignorance
  Of what each other mean,
And prate about an elephant
  Not one of them has seen!
                John Godfrey Saxe

Animal Fair

I went to the animal fair,
The birds and beasts were there.
The big baboon, by the light of the moon,

Was combing his auburn hair.
The monkey, he got drunk,
And sat on the elephant's trunk.
The elephant sneezed and fell on his knees,
And what became of the monk, the monk?

Unknown

Epitaph for a Funny Fellow

He always was one for a jeer and a jest,
　　And was given to iconoclasm;
His smile was sardonic, and seemed to suggest:
　　"Let others arouse 'em; I razz 'em!"

His phrases were likely to smolder and scald,
　　And act like a blister to bluster;
By the name of "buffoon" he was commonly
　　called,
　　Though possibly "jester" were juster.

We recently met; he was clouded in gloom;
　　His spirit was battered, embittered.
He asked me to chisel these words on his
　　tomb:
　　"The universe tottered; I tittered."

Morris Bishop

The Complete Misanthropist

I love to think of things I hate
  In moments of mopishness;
I hate people who sit up straight,
And youths who smirk about their "date,"
  And the dates who smirk no less.

I hate children who clutch and whine,
  And the arrogant, virtuous poor;
And critical connoisseurs of wine,
And everything that is called a shrine,
  And Art and Literature.

I hate eggs and I hate the hen;
  I hate the rooster, too.
I hate people who wield the pen,
I hate women and I hate men;
  And what's more, I hate you.

                    Morris Bishop

On Being a Woman

Why is it, when I am in Rome
I'd give an eye to be at home,
But when on native earth I be,
My soul is sick for Italy?

And why with you, my love, my lord,

Am I spectacularly bored,
Yet do you up and leave me — then
I scream to have you back again?

Dorothy Parker

the honey bee

the honey bee is sad and cross
and wicked as a weasel
and when she perches on you, boss,
she leaves a little measle

Don Marquis

Reverie

(Of a Gentleman of Sensibility at an Italian Table d'Hôte)

I

'Twas in a basement tobble d'hote
I met a sad sardine;
It was the saddest thing, I trow,
That I have ever seen,
With eyes so wan and lusterless
And frame so worn and lean

II

I gazed into its mournful eye,

Its eye gazed back at me;
I could not bear to eat a fish
That looked so mournfully.
"You, too, have suffered," I remarked,
And sighed with sympathy.

III

I am a staid, reflective man,
Of meditations grave;
The barber tells me all his griefs
When I go in to shave —
I wondered what this fish's life
Had been beneath the wave.

IV

Sometimes a very little thing
Will make my tears to flow —
"What was your life," I asked the fish,
"In those damp depths below?"
He did not answer me; words were
Too weak to bear his woe.

V

I am not always understood:
A dead bird on a hat
Moved me, one time, to weep upon
My hostess' neck — for that,
Although I only kissed her twice,
They kicked me from their flat.

VI

They did not realize I crave
Affection in my grief —
My bleeding heart oft yearns for love
As mustard yearns for beef —
"Poor fish," I said, "you lie so mute
Upon your lettuce leaf!"

VII

"If you could only speak, perhaps
The words might ease your pain!"
He looked at me as dull as look
The slag-heaps after rain
When one goes into Pittsburg town
Upon a railroad train.

VIII

"Perhaps from some great vessel's deck,
In mournful years long syne,
I've dropped into the moaning deep
A tear that mixed with thine —
What was your history before
We twain met here to dine?"

IX

Not one sign did he give to me
That showed he might have heard;
He only held me with his gaze,
He did not speak a word —
Did he withhold his confidence,

Or was it but deferred?

X

In either case, it made me mourn —
Though I am used to it;
Too often people stand aloof
From my more melting fit,
Too oft they fling and pierce me with
Their darts of cruel wit!

XI

I do recall a dream I had
In which I was full fed,
And when I woke at dawn I found
I'd eaten up my bed —
O gods! the bitter, witty words
That my landlady said!

XII

I do not care to write them down;
After the lapse of years
They still have power to trouble me;
They burn within my ears
As the harsh oaths of the Bedouins burn
Which the sad camel hears.

XIII

And what so sad as camels are
When through the desert dawn
A Pharaoh's mummy they descry

Lying his bier upon
With sand in his esophagus
And his ambition gone?

XIV

In the Smithsonian Institute
I knew a mummy mum
Who stared forever at the roof
All written and all glum,
As if he had four thousand years
Of colic in his tum;

XV

And I would stand as twilight fell
Beside his carven tomb
And strive to lighten with my songs
His long dyspeptic doom,
While skeletons of dinosaurs
Draw nearer in the gloom.

XVI

I never see a dinosaur
So patient and so mute
But that a song of pity springs
Unbidden to my lute —
He stayed a lizard, but he wished
To be a bird, poor brute!

XVII

I am so seldom understood!

Once, as my teardrops fell,
Upon a little lizard's head
Hard by a sylvan well
Coarse villagers came out in force
And haled me to a cell.

XVIII

I've never seen a lizard crawl
Along a rustic fence
But I've thought, "Poor helpless thing!
Some child may pluck you hence,
Thinking that you are edible —
They have so little sense!"

XIX

O little sad sardine, I find
This grief where'er I go!
And you have suffered likewise, for
Your manner tells me so —
O little sad sardine, I fear
Our world is full of woe!

Don Marquis

A Maxim Revised

Ladies, to this advice give heed —
In controlling men:
If at first you don't succeed,
Why, cry, cry again.

Unknown

Tobacco

Tobacco is a dirty weed:
   I like it.
It satisfies no normal need:
   I like it.
It makes you thin, it makes you lean,
It takes the hair right off your bean,
It's the worst darn stuff I've ever seen:
   I like it.

Graham Lee Hemminger

Liquor and Longevity

The horse and mule live thirty years
And nothing know of wines and beers.
The goat and sheep at twenty die
And never taste of Scotch or Rye.
The cow drinks water by the ton
And at eighteen is mostly done.
The dog at fifteen cashes in
Without the aid of rum and gin.
The cat in milk and water soaks
And then in twelve short years it croaks.
The modest, sober, bone-dry hen
Lays eggs for nogs, then dies at ten.

All animals are strictly dry:
They sinless live and swiftly die;
But sinful, ginful rum-soaked men
Survive for three score years and ten,
And some of them, a very few,
Stay pickled till they're ninety-two.

Unknown

Judged by the Company One Keeps

One night in late October,
When I was far from sober,
Returning with my load with manly pride,
My feet began to stutter,
So I lay down in the gutter,
And a pig came near and lay down by my side;
A lady passing by was heard to say:
"You can tell a man who boozes,
By the company he chooses,"
And the pig got up and slowly walked away.

Unknown

Trouble

Better never trouble Trouble
Until Trouble troubles you;
For you only make your trouble

Double-trouble when you do;
And the trouble — like a bubble —
That you're troubling about,
May be nothing but a cipher
With its rim rubbed out.

David Keppel

When I Get Time

When I get time —
   I know what I shall do:
I'll cut the leaves of all my books
   And read them through and through.

When I get time —
   I'll write some letters then
That I have owed for weeks and weeks
   To many, many men.

When I get time —
   I'll pay those calls I owe,
And with those bills, those countless bills,
   I will not be so slow.

When I get time —
   I'll regulate my life
In such a way that I may get
   Acquainted with my wife.

When I get time —
  Oh glorious dream of bliss!
A month, a year, ten years from now —
  But I can't finish this —
I've no more time.

Thomas L. Masson

Johnny's Hist'ry Lesson

I think of all the things at school
  A boy has got to do,
That studyin' hist'ry, as a rule,
  Is worst of all, don't you?
Of dates there are an awful sight,
An' though I study day an' night,
There's only one I've got just right —
  That's fourteen ninety-two.

Columbus crossed the Delaware
  In fourteen ninety-two;
We whipped the British, fair an' square,
  In fourteen ninety-two.
At Concord an' at Lexington
We kept the redcoats on the run
While the band played "Johnny Get Your
    Gun,"
  In fourteen ninety-two.

Pat Henry, with his dyin' breath —

In fourteen ninety-two —
Said "Gimme liberty or death!"
   In fourteen ninety-two.
An' Barbara Fritchie, so 'tis said,
Cried, "Shoot if you must this old gray head,
But I'd rather 'twould be your own instead!"
   In fourteen ninety-two.

The Pilgrims came to Plymouth Rock
   In fourteen ninety-two,
An' the Indians standin' on the dock
   Asked, "What are you goin' to do?"
An' they said, "We seek your harbor drear
That our children's children's children dear
May boast that their forefathers landed here
   In fourteen ninety-two."

Miss Pocahontas saved the life,
   In fourteen ninety-two,
Of John Smith, an' became his wife
   In fourteen ninety-two.
An' the Smith tribe started then an' there,
An' now there are John Smiths everywhere,
But they didn't have any Smiths to spare
   In fourteen ninety-two.

Kentucky was settled by Daniel Boone
   In fourteen ninety-two,
An' I think the cow jumped over the moon
   In fourteen ninety-two.

Ben Franklin flew his kite so high
He drew the lightnin' from the sky,
An' Washington couldn't tell a lie,
    In fourteen ninety-two.
                    Nixon Waterman

Investor's Soliloquy

To buy, or not to buy; that is the question:
Whether 'tis nobler in the mind to suffer
The slings and arrows of an outrageous market,
Or to take cash against a sea of troubles,
And by selling, end them. To buy, to keep —
No more; and by this keeping, to say we end
The bear trend and the thousand natural shocks
That stocks are heir to — 'tis a consummation
Devoutly to be wish'd — To buy, to keep —
To keep? Perchance on margin! Ay, there's the
    rub!
For in that margining what dreams may come,
When we have shuffled off our buying power,
Must give us pause. There's the respect
That makes calamity of so long a position.
For who would bear the whips and scorns of
    debit balances,
The broker's interest, the shorts' contumely,
The pangs of dispriz'd appreciation, the
    market's delay,
The insolence of bankers, and the spurns

That patient merit of the unworthy takes,
When he himself might the quietus make
With a bare short sale? Who would losses bear
To grunt and sweat under a falling market,
But that the dread of something after selling,
The undiscover'd rally — from whose bourn
No short seller returns, puzzles the will
And makes us rather bear those losses we have
Than fly to others that we know not of?
Thus ambivalence does make cowards of us
   all.
And thus the native hue of resolution
Is sicklied o'er with the pale cast of doubt
And enterprises of great pith and moment,
With this regard, their current turn awry,
And lose the name of profits.

                          Kenneth Ward

The Turtle

There are many who say that a dog has his
    day,
And a cat has a number of lives;
There are others who think that a lobster is
    pink,
And that bees never work in their hives.
There are fewer, of course, who insist that a
    horse
Has a horn and two humps on its head,
And a fellow who jests that a mare can build
    nests
Is as rare as a donkey that's red.
Yet in spite of all this, I have moments of
    bliss,
For I cherish a passion for bones,
And though doubtful of biscuits, I'm willing to
    risk it,
And love to chase rabbits and stones.
But my greatest delight is to take a good bite
At a calf that is plump and delicious;
And if I indulge in a bite at a bulge,
Let's hope you won't think me too vicious.

Ogden Nash

The Firefly

The firefly's flame
Is something for which science has no name.
I can think of nothing eerier
Than flying around with an unidentified glow
   on a person's posteerier.

Ogden Nash

The Pig

  The pig, if I am not mistaken,
  Supplies us sausage, ham, and bacon.
  Let others say his heart is big —
  I call it stupid of the pig.

Ogden Nash

I Never Even Suggested It

I know lots of men who are in love and lots of
    men who are married and lots of men who
    are both,
And to fall out with their loved ones is what
    all of them are most loth.
They are conciliatory at every opportunity,
Because all they want is serenity and a certain
    amount of impunity.
Yes, many the swain who has finally admitted
    that the earth is flat
Simply to sidestep a spat,
Many the masculine Positively or Absolutely
    which has been diluted to an If
Simply to avert a tiff,
Many the two-fisted executive whose domestic
    conversation is limited to a tactfully
    interpolated Yes,
And then he is amazed to find that he is being
    raked backwards over a bed of coals
    nevertheless.
These misguided fellows are under the
    impression that it takes two to make a
    quarrel, that you can sidestep a crisis by
    nonaggression and nonresistance,
Instead of removing yourself to a discreet
    distance.
Passivity can be a provoking *modus operandi;*
Consider the Empire and Gandhi.

Silence is golden, but sometimes invisibility is
    golder,
Because loved ones may not be able to make
    bricks without straw but often they don't
    need any straw to manufacture a bone to
    pick or blood in their eye or a chip for their
    soft white shoulder.
It is my duty, gentlemen, to inform you that
    women are dictators all, and I recommend to
    you this moral:
In real life it takes only one to make a quarrel.
                              Ogden Nash

The Sea-Gull

Hark to the whimper of the sea-gull;
He weeps because he's not an ea-gull.
Suppose you were, you silly sea-gull,
Could you explain it to your she-gull?
                              Ogden Nash

Song of the Open Road

I think that I shall never see
A billboard lovely as a tree.
Perhaps, unless the billboards fall,
I'll never see a tree at all.

Ogden Nash

Various Themes

Song

Go and catch a falling star,
  Get with child a mandrake root,
Tell me where all past years are,
  Or who cleft the Devil's foot;
Teach me to hear mermaids singing,
Or to keep off envy's stinging,
    And find
    What wind
Serves to advance an honest mind.

If thou be'st born to strange sights,
  Things invisible to see,
Ride ten thousand days and nights
  Till Age snow white hairs on thee;
Thou, when thou return'st, wilt tell me
All strange wonders that befell thee,
    And swear
    No where
Lives a woman true and fair.

If thou find'st one, let me know;
  Such a pilgrimage were sweet.
Yet do not; I would not go,
  Though at next door we might meet.

Though she were true when you met her,
And last till you write your letter,
　　Yet she
　　Will be
False, ere I come, to two or three.

John Donne

A Little Learning Is a Dangerous Thing

A little learning is a dangerous thing;
Drink deep, or taste not the Pierian spring:
There shallow draughts intoxicate the brain,
And drinking largely sobers us again.
Fired at first sight with what the Muse imparts,
In fearless youth we tempt the heights of Arts,
While from the bounded level of our mind,
Short views we take, nor see the lengths
　　behind;
But more advanced, behold with strange
　　surprise
New distant scenes of endless science rise!
So pleased at first the towering Alps we try,
Mount o'er the vales, and seem to tread the
　　sky,
Th' eternal snows appear already past,
And the first clouds and mountains seem the
　　last;
But, those attained, we tremble to survey
The growing labors of the lengthened way,

Th' increasing prospect tires our wandering
  eyes,
Hills peep o'er hills, and Alps on Alps arise!
                    (From *Essay on Criticism, II*)
                                    Alexander Pope

Kubla Khan

In Xanadu did Kubla Khan
  A stately pleasure-dome decree:
Where Alph, the sacred river, ran
Through caverns measureless to man
  Down to a sunless sea
So twice five miles of fertile ground
With walls and towers were girdled round:
And here were gardens bright with sinuous
    rills,
Where blossomed many an incense-bearing
    tree,
And here were forests ancient as the hills,
Enfolding sunny spots of greenery.

But oh! that deep romantic chasm which
    slanted
Down the green hill athwart a cedarn cover!
A savage place; as holy and enchanted
As e'er beneath a waning moon was haunted
By woman wailing for her demon-lover!
And from this chasm, with ceaseless turmoil
    seething,

As if this earth in fast thick pants were
        breathing,
A mighty fountain momently was forced,
Amid whose swift half-intermitted burst
Huge fragments vaulted like rebounding hail,
Or chaffy grain beneath the thresher's flail:
And 'mid these dancing rocks at once and ever
It flung up momently the sacred river.
Five miles meandering with a mazy motion
Through wood and dale the sacred river ran,
Then reached the caverns measureless to man,
And sank in tumult to a lifeless ocean:
And 'mid this tumult Kubla heard from far
Ancestral voices prophesying war!

   The shadow of the dome of pleasure
   Floated midway on the waves;
   Where was heard the mingled measure
   From the fountain and the caves.
It was a miracle of rare device,
A sunny pleasure-dome with caves of ice!

   A damsel with a dulcimer
   In a vision once I saw:
   It was an Abyssinian maid,
   And on her dulcimer she played,
   Singing of Mount Abora.
   Could I revive within me
   Her symphony and song,
   To such a deep delight 'twould win me,

That with music loud and long,
I would build that dome in air,
That sunny dome! those caves of ice!
And all who heard should see them there,
And all should cry, Beware! Beware!
His flashing eyes, his floating hair!
Weave a circle round him thrice,
And close your eyes with holy dread,
For he on honey-dew hath fed,
And drunk the milk of Paradise.

Samuel Taylor Coleridge

Ozymandias

I met a traveler from an antique land
Who said: Two vast and trunkless legs of stone
Stand in the desert. Near them, on the sand,
Half sunk, a shattered visage lies, whose frown
And wrinkled lip and sneer of cold command
Tell that its sculptor well those passions read
Which yet survive, stamped on these lifeless
    things,
The hand that mocked them and the heart that
    fed;
And on the pedestal these words appear:
"My name is Ozymandias, king of kings:
Look on my works, ye Mighty, and despair!"
Nothing beside remains. Round the decay

Of that colossal wreck, boundless and bare,
The lone and level sands stretch far away.
Percy Bysshe Shelley

Ode on a Grecian Urn

Thou still unravish'd bride of quietness,
   Thou foster-child of silence and slow time,
Sylvan historian, who canst thus express
   A flowery tale more sweetly than our rhyme:
What leaf-fring'd legend haunts about thy shape
   Of deities or mortals, or of both
      In Tempe or the dales of Arcady?
    What men or gods are these? What maidens
      loth?
What mad pursuit? What struggle to escape?
    What pipes and timbrels? What wild
      ecstacy?

Heard melodies are sweet, but those unheard
   Are sweeter; therefore, ye soft pipes, play
      on;
Not to the sensual ear, but, more endear'd,
   Pipe to the spirit ditties of no tone:
Fair youth, beneath the trees, thou canst not
      leave
   Thy song, nor ever can those trees be bare;
    Bold Lover, never, never canst thou kiss,
Though winning near the goal — yet, do not

grieve;
She cannot fade, though thou hast not thy
bliss,
For ever wilt thou love, and she be fair!

Ah, happy, happy boughs! that cannot shed
Your leaves, nor ever bid the Spring adieu;
And, happy melodist, unwearièd,
For ever piping songs for ever new;
More happy love! more happy, happy love!
For ever warm and still to be enjoy'd,
For ever panting, and for ever young;
All breathing human passion far above,
That leaves a heart high-sorrowful and
cloy'd,
A burning forehead, and a parching
tongue.

Who are these coming to the sacrifice?
To what green altar, O mysterious priest,
Lead'st thou that heifer lowing at the skies,
And all her silken flanks with garlands
drest?
What little town by river or sea shore,
Or mountain-built with peaceful citadel,
Is emptied of this folk, this pious morn?
And, little town, thy streets for evermore
Will silent be; and not a soul to tell
Why thou art desolate, can e'er return.

O Attic shape! Fair attitude! with brede
  Of marble men and maidens overwrought,
With forest branches and the trodden weed;
  Thou, silent form, dost tease us out of
      thought
As doth eternity. Cold Pastoral!
  When old age shall this generation waste,
    Thou shalt remain, in midst of other woe
Than ours, a friend to man, to whom thou
      say'st,
  "Beauty is truth, truth beauty — that is all
    Ye know on earth, and all ye need to
      know."

John Keats

On First Looking into Chapman's Homer

Much have I travelled in the realms of gold,
  And many goodly states and kingdoms seen;
  Round many western islands have I been
Which bards in fealty to Apollo hold.
Oft of one wide expanse had I been told
  That deep-browed Homer ruled as his
    demesne:
  Yet did I never breathe its pure serene
Till I heard Chapman speak out loud and bold:
Then felt I like some watcher of the skies
  When a new planet swims into his ken;
Or like stout Cortez, when with eagle eyes

He stared at the Pacific — and all his men
Looked at each other with a wild surmise —
Silent, upon a peak in Darien.

John Keats

Ulysses

It little profits that an idle king,
By this still hearth, among these barren crags,
Matched with an aged wife, I mete and dole
Unequal laws unto a savage race,
That hoard, and sleep, and feed, and know not
    me.
I cannot rest from travel: I will drink
Life to lees: all times I have enjoyed
Greatly, have suffered greatly, both with those
That loved me, and alone; on shore, and when
Through scudding drifts the rainy Hyades
Vext the dim sea. I am become a name;
For always roaming with a hungry heart
Much have I seen and known: cities of men
And manners, climates, councils, governments,
Myself not least, but honored of them all, —
And drunk delight of battle with my peers,
Far on the ringing plains of windy Troy.
I am a part of all that I have met;
Yet all experience is an arch wherethrough
Gleams that untraveled world, whose margin
    fades

For ever and for ever when I move.
How dull it is to pause, to make an end,
To rust unburnished, not to shine in use!
As though to breathe were life. Life piled on
   life
Were all too little, and of one to me
Little remains: but every hour is saved
From that eternal silence, something more,
A bringer of new things; and vile it were
For some three suns to store and hoard myself,
And this gray spirit yearning in desire
To follow knowledge, like a sinking star,
Beyond the utmost bound of human thought.
   This is my son, mine own Telemachus,
To whom I leave the scepter and the isle —
Well-loved of me, discerning to fulfill
This labor, by slow prudence to make mild
A rugged people, and through soft degrees
Subdue them to the useful and the good.
Most blameless is he, centered in the sphere
Of common duties, decent not to fail
In offices of tenderness, and pay
Meet adoration to my household gods,
When I am gone. He works his work, I mine.
   There lies the port: the vessel puffs her sail:
There gloom the dark broad seas. My
   mariners,
Souls that have toiled, and wrought, and
   thought with me —
That ever with a frolic welcome took

The thunder and the sunshine, and opposed
Free hearts, free foreheads — you and I are
   old;
Old age hath yet his honor and his toil;
Death closes all: but something ere the end,
Some work of noble note, may yet be done,
Not unbecoming men that strove with Gods.
The lights begin to twinkle from the rocks:
The long day wanes: the slow moon climbs:
   the deep
Moans round with many voices. Come, my
   friends,
'Tis not too late to seek a newer world.
Push off, and sitting well in order smite
The sounding furrows; for my purpose holds
To sail beyond the sunset, and the baths
Of all the western stars, until I die.
It may be that the gulfs will wash us down:
It may be we shall touch the Happy Isles,
And see the great Achilles, whom we knew.
Though much is taken, much abides; and
   though
We are not now that strength which in old days
Moved earth and heaven, that which we are,
   we are, —
One equal temper of heroic hearts,
Made weak by time and fate, but strong in will
To strive, to seek, to find, and to yield.

Alfred Tennyson

The Bells

I

Hear the sledges with the bells,
   Silver bells!
What a world of merriment their melody
     foretells!
How they tinkle, tinkle, tinkle,
   In the icy air of night!
While the stars that oversprinkle
All the heavens seem to twinkle
   With a crystalline delight;
   Keeping time, time, time,
   In a sort of Runic rhyme,
To the tintinabulation that so musically wells
  From the bells, bells, bells, bells,
    Bells, bells, bells —
From the jingling and the tinkling of the bells.

II

Hear the mellow wedding bells,
   Golden bells!
What a world of happiness their harmony
     foretells!
  Through the balmy air of night
  How they ring out their delight!
  From the molten-golden notes,
   And all in tune,
  What a liquid ditty floats
To the turtle-dove that listens, while she gloats

On the moon!
Oh, from out the sounding cells,
What a gush of euphony voluminously wells!
How it swells!
How it dwells
On the future; how it tells
Of the rapture that impels
To the swinging and the ringing
Of the bells, bells, bells,
Of the bells, bells, bells, bells,
Bells, bells, bells —
To the rhyming and the chiming of the bells!

III

Hear the loud alarum bells —
Brazen bells!
What a tale of terror, now, their turbulency
tells
In the startled ear of night
How they scream out their affright!
Too much horrified to speak,
They can only shriek, shriek,
Out of tune,
In a clamorous appealing to the mercy of the
fire,
In a mad expostulation with the deaf and
frantic fire.
Leaping higher, higher, higher,
With a desperate desire,
And a resolute endeavor

Now, now to sit, or never,
By the side of the pale-faced moon.
Oh, the bells, bells, bells!
What a tale their terror tells
Of despair!
How they clang, and clash, and roar!
What a horror they outpour
On the bosom of the palpitating air!
Yet the ear it fully knows,
By the twanging,
And the clanging,
How the danger ebbs and flows;
Yet the ear distinctly tells,
In the jangling,
And the wrangling,
How the danger sinks and swells,
By the sinking or the swelling in the anger of
the bells;
Of the bells —
Of the bells, bells, bells, bells,
Bells, bells, bells —
In the clamor and the clangor of the bells!

IV

Hear the tolling of the bells,
Iron bells!
What a world of solemn thought their melody
compels!
In the silence of the night,
How we shiver with affright

At the melancholy menace of their tone!
    For every sound that floats
    From the rust within their throats,
      Is a groan.
And the people — ah, the people,
They that dwell up in the steeple,
      All alone.
And who tolling, tolling, tolling,
   In that muffled monotone,
Feel a glory in so rolling
    On the human heart a stone —
They are neither man nor woman,
They are neither brute nor human,
      They are ghouls:
And their king it is who tolls;
And he rolls, rolls, rolls,
      Rolls
A paean from the bells!
And his merry bosom swells
With the paean of the bells!
And he dances, and he yells;
    Keeping time, time, time,
    In a sort of Runic rhyme,
To the paean of the bells,
     Of the bells;
    Keeping time, time, time,
    In a sort of Runic rhyme,
To the throbbing of the bells;
Of the bells, bells, bells —
To the sobbing of the bells;

Keeping time, time, time,
In a happy Runic rhyme,
To the rolling of the bells;
Of the bells, bells, bells —
To the tolling of the bells,
Of the bells, bells, bells, bells,
Bells, bells, bells —
To the moaning and the groaning of the bells.

Edgar Allan Poe

Eldorado

Gaily bedight,
A gallant knight,
In sunshine and in shadow,
Had journeyed long,
Singing a song,
In search of Eldorado.

But he grew old —
This knight so bold —
And o'er his heart a shadow
Fell as he found
No spot of ground
Tha. looked like Eldorado.

And, as his strength
Failed him at length,
He met a pilgrim shadow —

"Shadow," said he
"Where can it be —
This land of Eldorado?"

"Over the mountains
Of the moon,
Down the valley of the shadow,
  Ride, boldly ride,"
The shade replied, —
"If you seek for Eldorado!"
                              Edgar Allan Poe

The Female of the Species

1911

When the Himalayan peasant meets the he-bear
  in his pride,
He shouts to scare the monster, who will often
  turn aside;
But the she-bear thus accosted rends the
  peasant tooth and nail,
For the female of the species is more deadly
  than the male.

When Nag the basking cobra hears the careless
  foot of man,
He will sometimes wriggle sideways and avoid
  it as he can;
But his mate makes no such motion where she
  camps beside the trail,
For the female of the species is more deadly
  than the male.

When the early Jesuit fathers preached to
  Hurons and Choctaws,
They prayed to be delivered from the
  vengeance of the squaws.
'Twas the women, not the warriors, turned
  those stark enthusiasts pale,
For the female of the species is more deadly
  than the male.

Man's timid heart is bursting with the things he
  must not say,
For the Woman that God gave him isn't his to
  give away;
But when the hunter meets with husband, each
  confirms the other's tale —
The female of the species is more deadly than
  the male.

Man, a bear in most relations — worm and
  savage otherwise, —
Man propounds negotiations, Man accepts the
  compromise.
Very rarely will he squarely push the logic of a
  fact
To its ultimate conclusion in unmitigated act.

Fear, or foolishness, impels him, ere he lay the
  wicked low,
To concede some form of trial even to his
  fiercest foe.
Mirth obscene diverts his anger! Doubt and
  Pity oft perplex
Him in dealing with an issue — to the scandal
  of The Sex!

But the Woman that God gave him, every fibre
  of her frame
Proves her launched for one sole issue, armed
  and engined for the same;

And to serve that single issue, lest the
    generations fail,
The female of the species must be deadlier than
    the male.

She who faces Death by torture for each life
    beneath her breast
May not deal in doubt or pity — must not
    swerve for fact or jest.
These be purely male diversions — not in these
    her honour dwells.
She the Other Law we live by, is that Law and
    nothing else.

She can bring no more to living than the
    powers that make her great
And the Mother of the Infant and the Mistress
    of the Mate!
And when Babe and Man are lacking and she
    strides unclaimed to claim
Her right as femme (and baron), her equipment
    is the same.

She is wedded to convictions — in default of
    grosser ties;
Her contentions are her children, Heaven help
    him who denies! —
He will meet no suave discussion, but the
    instant, white-hot, wild,
Wakened female of the species warring as for

spouse and child.

Unprovoked and awful changes — even so the
   she-bear fights,
Speech that drips, corrodes, and poisons —
   even so the cobra bites,
Scientific vivisection of one nerve till it is raw,
And the victim writhes in anguish — like the
   Jesuit with the squaw!

So it comes that Man the coward, when he
   gathers to confer
With her fellow-braves in council, dare not
   leave a place for her
Where, at war with Life and Conscience, he
   uplifts his erring hands
To some God of Abstract Justice — which no
   woman understands.

And Man knows it! Knows, moreover, that the
   Woman that God gave him
Must command but may not govern — shall
   enthral but not enslave him.
And She knows, because She warns him, and
   Her instincts never fail,
That the Female of Her Species is more deadly
   than the Male.

Rudyard Kipling

There Is No Frigate Like a Book

There is no Frigate like a Book
To take us Lands away
Nor any Coursers like a Page
Of prancing Poetry —
This Traverse may the poorest take
Without oppress of Toll —
How frugal is the Chariot
That bears the Human soul.

Emily Dickinson

Patterns

I walk down the garden-paths,
And all the daffodils
Are blowing, and the bright blue squills
I walk down the patterned garden-paths
In my stiff, brocaded gown
With my powdered hair and jeweled fan,
I too am a rare
Pattern. As I wander down
The garden-paths.

My dress is richly figured,
And the train
Makes a pink and silver stain
On the gravel, and the thrift
Of the borders.

426

Just a plate of current fashion,
Tripping by in high-heeled, ribboned shoes.
Not a softness anywhere about me,
Only whalebone and brocade.
And I sink on a seat in the shade
Of a lime-tree. For my passion
Wars against the stiff brocade.
The daffodils and squills
Flutter in the breeze
As they please.
And I weep;
For the lime-tree is in blossom
And one small flower has dropped upon my
    bosom.

And the plashing of waterdrops
In the marble fountain
Comes down the garden-paths.
The dripping never stops.
Underneath my stiffened gown
Is the softness of a woman bathing in a marble
    basin,
A basin in the midst of hedges grown
So thick, she cannot see her lover hiding,
But she guesses he is near,
And the sliding of the water
Seems the stroking of a dear
Hand upon her.
What is Summer in a fine brocaded gown!
I should like to see it lying in a heap upon the

ground.
All the pink and silver crumpled up on the
  ground.

I would be the pink and silver as I ran along
  the paths,
And he would stumble after,
Bewildered by my laughter.
I should see the sun flashing from his sword-
  hilt and the buckles on his shoes.
I would choose
To lead him in a maze along the patterned
  paths,
A bright and laughing maze for my heavy-
  booted lover.
Till he caught me in the shade,
And the buttons of his waistcoat bruised my
  body as he clasped me,
Aching, melting, unafraid.
With the shadows of the leaves and the
  sundrops,
And the plopping of the waterdrops,
All about us in the open afternoon —
I am very like to swoon
With the weight of this brocade,
For the sun sifts through the shade.

Underneath the fallen blossom
In my bosom
Is a letter I have hid.

It was brought to me this morning by a rider
    from the Duke.
"Madam, we regret to inform you that Lord
    Hartwell
Died in action Thursday sen'night."
As I read it in the white, morning sunlight,
The letters squirmed like snakes.
"Any answer, Madam?" said my footman.
"No," I told him.
"See that the messenger takes some
    refreshment.
"No, no answer."
And I walked into the garden,
Up and down the patterned paths,
In my stiff, correct brocade.
The blue and yellow flowers stood up proudly
    in the sun,
Each one.
I stood upright too,
Held rigid to the pattern
By the stiffness of my gown;
Up and down I walked,
Up and down.

In a month he would have been my husband.
In a month, here, underneath this lime,
We would have broke the pattern;
He for me, and I for him,
He as Colonel, I as Lady,
On this shady seat.

He had a whim
That sunlight carried blessing.
And I answered, "It shall be as you have
   said."
Now he is dead.

In Summer and in Winter I shall walk
Up and down
The patterned garden-paths
In my stiff, brocaded gown.
The squills and daffodils
Will give place to pillared roses, and to asters,
   and to snow.
I shall go
Up and down
In my gown.
Gorgeously arrayed,
Boned and stayed.
And the softness of my body will be guarded
   from embrace
By each button, hook, and lace.
For the man who should loose me is dead,
Fighting with the Duke in Flanders,
In a pattern called a war.
Christ! What are patterns for?

Amy Lowell

Leda and the Swan

A sudden blow: the great wings beating still
Above the staggering girl, her thighs caressed
By the dark webs, her nape caught in his bill,
He holds her helpless breast upon his breast.

How can those terrified vague fingers push
The feathered glory from her loosening thighs?
And how can body, laid in that white rush,
But feel the strange heart beating where it lies?

A shudder in the loins engenders there
The broken wall, the burning roof and tower
And Agamemnon dead.
                    Being so caught up,
So mastered by the brute blood of the air,
Did she put on his knowledge with his power
Before the indifferent beak could let her drop?

William Butler Yeats

Sailing to Byzantium

That is no country for old men. The young
In one another's arms, birds in the trees,
— Those dying generations — at their song,
The salmon-falls, the mackerel-crowded seas,
Fish, flesh, or fowl, commend all summer long
Whatever is begotten, born, and dies.

Caught in that sensual music all neglect
Monuments of unaging intellect.

An aged man is but a paltry thing,
A tattered coat upon a stick, unless
Soul clap its hands and sing, and louder sing
For every tatter in its mortal dress,
Nor is there singing school but studying
Monuments of its own magnificence;
And therefore I have sailed the seas and come
To the holy city of Byzantium.

O sages standing in God's holy fire
As in the gold mosaic of a wall,
Come from the holy fire, perne in a gyre,
And be the singing-masters of my soul.
Consume my heart away; sick with desire
And fastened to a dying animal
It knows not what it is; and gather me
Into the artifice of eternity.

Once out of nature I shall never take
My bodily form from any natural thing,
But such a form as Grecian goldsmiths make
Of hammered gold and gold enameling
To keep a drowsy Emperor awake;
Or set upon a golden bough to sing
To lords and ladies of Byzantium
Of what is past, or passing, or to come.

William Butler Yeats

Recuerdo

We were very tired, we were very merry—
We had gone back and forth all night on the
   ferry.
It was bare and bright, and smelled like a
   stable —
But we looked into a fire, we leaned across a
   table,
We lay on a hilltop underneath the moon;
And the whistles kept blowing, and the dawn
   came soon.

We were very tired, we were very merry —
We had gone back and forth all night on the
   ferry.
And you ate an apple, and I ate a pear,
From a dozen of each we had bought
   somewhere;
And the sky went wan, and the wind came
   cold,
And the sun rose dripping, a bucketful of gold.

We were very tired, we were very merry,
We had gone back and forth all night on the
   ferry.
We hailed, "Good morrow, mother!" to a
   shawl-covered head,
And bought a morning paper, which neither of
   us read;

And she wept, "God bless you!" for the
    apples and pears,
And we gave her all our money but our
    subway fares.
Edna St. Vincent Millay

First Fig

My candle burns at both ends;
    It will not last the night;
But, ah, my foes, and, oh, my friends —
    It gives a lovely light!
Edna St. Vincent Millay

anyone lived in a pretty how town

anyone lived in a pretty how town
(with up so floating many bells down)
spring summer autumn winter
he sang his didn't he danced his did.

Women and men(both little and small)
cared for anyone not at all
they sowed their isn't they reaped their same
sun moon stars rain

children guessed(but only a few
and down they forgot as up they grew

autumn winter spring summer)
that noone loved him more by more

when by now and tree by leaf
she laughed his joy she cried his grief
bird by snow and stir by still
anyone's any was all to her

someones married their everyones
laughed their cryings and did their dance
(sleep wake hope and then)they
said their nevers they slept their dream

stars rain sun moon
(and only the snow can begin to explain
how children are apt to forget to remember
with up so floating many bells down)

one day anyone died i guess
(and noone stooped to kiss his face)
busy folk buried them side by side
little by little and was by was

all by all and deep by deep
and more by more they dream their sleep
noone and anyone earth by april
wish by spirit and if by yes.

Women and men(both dong and ding)
summer autumn winter spring

reaped their sowing and went their came
sun moon stars rain

e. e. cummings

Mending Wall

Something there is that doesn't love a wall,
That sends the frozen-ground-swell under it,
And spills the upper boulders in the sun;
And makes gaps even two can pass abreast.
The work of hunters is another thing:
I have come after them and made repair
Where they have left not one stone on a stone,
But they would have the rabbit out of hiding,
To please the yelping dogs. The gaps I mean,
No one has seen them made or heard them
    made,
But at spring mending-time we find them
    there.
I let my neighbor know beyond the hill;
And on a day we meet to walk the line
And set the wall between us once again.
We keep the wall between us as we go.
To each the boulders that have fallen to each.
And some are loaves and some so nearly balls
We have to use a spell to make them balance:
"Stay where you are until our backs are
    turned!"

We wear our fingers rough with handling
  them.
Oh, just another kind of outdoor game,
One on a side. It comes to little more:
There where it is we do not need the wall:
He is all pine and I am apple-orchard.
My apple trees will never get across
And eat the cones under his pines, I tell him.
He only says, "Good fences make good
  neighbors."
Spring is the mischief in me, and I wonder
If I could put a notion in his head:
"*Why* do they make good neighbors? Isn't it
Where there are cows? But here there are no
  cows.
Before I built a wall I'd ask to know
What I was walling in or walling out,
And to whom I was like to give offence.
Something there is that doesn't love a wall,
That wants it down!" I could say "elves" to
  him,
But it's not elves exactly, and I'd rather
He said it for himself. I see him there,
Bringing a stone grasped firmly by the top
In each hand, like an old stone savage armed.
He moves in darkness, as it seems to me,
Not of woods only and the shade of trees.
He will not go behind his father's saying,
And he likes having thought of it so well

He says again, "Good fences make good neighbors."

Robert Frost

Ars Poetica

A poem should be palpable and mute
As a globed fruit

Dumb
As old medallions to the thumb

Silent as the sleeve-worn stone
Of casement ledges where the moss has
  grown —

A poem should be wordless
As the flight of birds

A poem should be motionless in time
As the moon climbs

Leaving, as the moon releases
Twig by twig the night-entangled trees,

Leaving, as the moon behind the winter leaves,
Memory by memory the mind —

A poem should be motionless in time
As the moon climbs

A poem should be equal to:
Not true

For all the history of grief
An empty doorway and a maple leaf

For love
The leaning grasses and two lights above the
sea —

A poem should not mean
But be.

Archibald MacLeish

Index of Authors

Index of Titles

449

Index of First Lines

Listen, my children, and you shall hear, 24
Lord, make me an instrument of Your peace, 293
Love is not all: it is not meat nor drink, 125
Miniver Cheevy, child of scorn, 61
Much have I travelled in the realms of gold, 412
My candle burns at both ends, 434
My childhood's home I see again, 228
My heart leaps up when I behold A Rainbow in the
    sky, 132
My long two-pointed ladder's sticking through a tree, 174
My love is like to ice, and I to fire, 81
No coward soul is mine, 332
Not like the brazen giant of Greek fame, 277
Now as I was young and easy under the apple
    boughs, 180
Now what is Love, I pray thee, tell?, 81
O Captain! my Captain! our fearful trip is done, 275
O God, the Rock of Ages, 303
O my aged Uncle Arly!, 362
O my luve is like a red, red rose, 98
O what a tangled web we weave, 379
O where hae ye been, Lord Randal, my son?, 3
O who will walk a mile with me, 113
O wild West Wind, thou breath of Autumn's being, 136
O world, thou choosest not the better part!, 317
Often I think of the beautiful town, 198
Oh, to be in England, 152
Oh what can ail thee, knight-at-arms!, 8
Oh, young Lochinvar is come out of the west, 4
On the white throat of the useless passion, 123
Once this soft turf, this rivulet's sands, 263
Once upon a midnight dreary, while I pondered, weak
    and weary, 13